# THE STUFF OF LIFE

## Public Health
# IN EDWARDIAN BRITAIN

**W. Hatchett, S. Spear, J. and J. Stewart,
A. Greenwell and D. Clapham**

CIEH
Association of Port Health Authorities
University of Greenwich

First published in 2012 by CIEH

British Library Cataloguing in Publication Data. A catalogue
record for this book is available from the British Library.

ISBN 978-1-906989-56-9

Design by Jon Heal

Printed and bound by Highworth Press Ltd

# CONTENTS

# FOREWORD

As this absorbing book shows, the development of environmental and public health in Edwardian Britain makes a fascinating study. Society was changing. It was a time of radical thought, and recognition by some that the old order could not continue, even if reforms instigated by the likes of Sir Edwin Chadwick and Sir John Simon had led to improved public health. There was still the notion of the deserving and undeserving poor, however. Even the late-Victorian philanthropists such as were providing accommodation for the "working classes" focussed on those who in their eyes were "deserving" and would conform to their paternalistic approach. For example, as this book shows, Octavia Hill, like many of her generation of social reformers and social innovators, was opposed to any large-scale intervention by the state (national or local) in welfare.

Hill's system of housing provision and management was based on closely managing not only buildings but tenants also, as she insisted that it was not possible to deal with the people and their houses separately. Whatever our modern view of this approach (and we do appear increasingly to be reverting to notions of the deserving and undeserving) advances were being made by people who would speak out and take action to deal with what were seen as ills of society that affected public health. There was also the recognition that some form of planning was required and the first moves towards what we now consider to be planning began at this time, even if the New Towns Act and the Town and Country Planning Act did not appear until after the Second World War.

It was another Edwardian, George Bernard Shaw, who said that: "The reasonable man (sic) adapts himself to the world; the unreasonable one persists in trying to adapt the world to himself. Therefore, all progress depends on the unreasonable man." This book provides much evidence to support that notion. Certainly, progress in environmental health terms was attributable to some strong characters and one wonders whether such characters exist today – those who are willing to stand against vested interests. It is interesting that GBS refers to the "unreasonable man" but this books shows that in Edwardian Britain, women were playing a crucial part in highlighting and dealing with public health problems and were not afraid to be "political". It is thus somewhat ironic that only now in the 21$^{st}$ century does the Chartered Institute of Environmental Health (the professional body for environmental health officers) have its first woman president.

Many aspects of civil society may have changed in the past 100 years (much attributable to two world wars and the aftermath including the demise of the post-war consensus) but this book can still teach modern environmental health practitioners and others some valuable lessons. Perhaps at this time we need to be encouraging public and environmental health workers to be assertive in arguing for more coherent, stronger action to address health inequalities and to highlight the problems they encounter on the ground. It is not their role to act as gatekeepers, deciding who is or is not deserving of their interventions. Rather than work to centrally determined priorities, if localism has any meaning, they should be focussing on those whose health is most at risk and health inequity. All the evidence indicates that the more unequal a country is, the greater are the health inequalities and indeed the unhealthier the country is as a whole. After many years of the gap between the top and bottom 10 per cent of earners narrowing, it is again on an upward trajectory towards Edwardian levels. Public and environmental health workers may not be able to address wealth inequality but they can address health inequity. At a time when "deficit reduction" is the excuse for expenditure cuts that disproportionately affect those on lowest incomes, it is perhaps useful to put this deficit into perspective.

In 1852, public net debt as percentage of gross domestic product was 129 per cent. In 1918, it was 114.5 per cent, in 1945, 216 per cent and, in 1962, almost 100 per cent. In 2011, it was 60 per cent (from 36 per cent in 2008) and so there is no reason why public health should suffer as a consequence of public debt – it is indeed a false economy. It was Martin Luther King who said: "History will have to record that the greatest tragedy of this period of social transition was not the strident clamour of the bad people, but the appalling silence of the good people." This book shows how many good people 100 years ago were not silent.

*Stephen Battersby, past president,*
*Chartered Institute of Environmental Health*

# ACKNOWLEDGEMENTS

Many people made the authors' task easier and more pleasurable, whether by commenting on early plans for the book, contributing treasured historical materials, advising on chapters or facilitating access to specialised collections or libraries. We should particularly like to acknowledge the following: John Ambrose of the Port Health Authority of London (for his help in supplying contacts); Graham Butterworth (for loaning annual public heath reports and other materials from Manchester); Bill Carey (for permission to reproduce family photographs, general guidance and loan of books from his inspirational collection); Rob Couch (for his advice and comments); Laurence H. Dettman of Hull and Goole Port Health Authority (for material on the conditions for migrants a century ago); First Garden City Heritage Museum (for permission to reproduce the three magnets diagram and information provided on visits to Letchworth, Hertfordshire); Tina Garrity (for her support and help in accessing the invaluable CIEH library); Julia Hayden of London Port Health Authority (for her assistance in checking records); Andy Hopson (for making available his history of Falmouth and Truro Port Health Authority); David Jones of Portsmouth and Tony Morris (for pointing us to the right people in port health); Tony Lewis (for reading and commenting on the manuscript); John Major (for help with source material on Bradford); Christopher Rankin, Mercola Douglas and the team at Mersey Port Health Authority (for their co-operation and hospitality); staff at the Royal College of Nursing Library archives (for providing original source materials on health visiting); Ed Wingfield of Tyne Port Health Authority (for supplying source materials and historical photographs); and the staff of the Women's Library (for finding valuable material on women pioneers in public health).

# INTRODUCTION

*Public health: The science and art of preventing disease, prolonging life and promoting health through the organised efforts of society.*
*Sir Donald Acheson, Chief Medical Officer, 1988*

The stuff of life is simple. It's what you go to the shops for when there is nothing left in the refrigerator or cupboard – milk, bread, bacon, margarine, tea, sugar. It's also the places where you work and live, and the air that you breathe. The stuff of life has not changed much since Edwardian times except that, 100 years ago, the working class diet did not stray far beyond simple staples – except on Sundays, when cheap cuts of meat came into their own for the weekly roast.

For more than 150 years, environmental health officers (known in Edwardian times as Inspectors of Nuisance or Sanitary Inspectors) have been responsible for ensuring the integrity of the stuff of life. This unsung male and female workforce inspected abattoirs and dairies, where corners were often cut in the never-ending quest for profit; sampled foodstuffs for contamination or adulteration; dealt with complaints about sub-standard food and housing; went into factories and workshops; investigated nuisance from smoke, stench, filth or noise; and were much-preoccupied with damp, mould and blocked drains. In short, they attempted to remove the causes of outbreaks of infectious and contagious disease and the sheer grinding toll of poverty.

Today, many members of a professional body, the Chartered Institute of Environmental Health, still fulfil this rewarding role, although some of the issues they deal with have changed. Relatively, they are paid better than their Edwardian predecessors, who would have regarded £100 a year as a decent salary and often lacked security of tenure. But it is fair to say that they are motivated more by a sense of vocation and public duty than the pursuit of wealth.

Food poisoning should never be trivialised – it can kill. But in Edwardian times, it was only one of a series of issues that sanitary inspectors were employed to address. Illnesses that those of us born in the 1950s can still remember as a feature of childhood – scarlet fever, hooping cough and measles – were a major cause of mortality. Diphtheria and polio killed in large numbers; smallpox (the first disease to be tackled by a national vaccination programme) also carried away thousands in sporadic outbreaks, especially where people lived close together.

The potentially fatal diseases principally caused by contaminated water, such as cholera and typhoid (often called enteric fever), had caused terror to Victorian Britain. Asiatic cholera, an appalling disease that turned the skin a bluish-grey and could kill in hours, was carefully mapped as it crossed the world, arriving on the Durham coast, like a medieval plague, in 1831. By 1910, the water-borne diseases had largely been beaten back through the simple segregation of sewage and drinking water – a measure that had been adopted for intuitive reasons even before their causes were properly understood.

Typhus, spread by ticks, was also tailing away; the worst horrors of overcrowded urban housing had been ameliorated, if not removed, by by-laws and housing and planning legislation. But tuberculosis – the largest killer of the 19th and 20th centuries – still stalked the land. It occurred wherever people lived close together, sneezing, coughing and spitting. There was no cure. And the bacillus that caused the disease arrived daily to towns and cities, in milk churns, to harvest thousands of fresh victims. This unnecessary scourge persisted long after it was known that pasteurisation rendered infected milk safe (see chapter seven).

The poorest who were gravely ill or destitute largely had recourse to the workhouse, an institution yet to be rendered obsolete by benefits and insurance schemes introduced by Liberal governments after 1906. Skilled writers, like Charles Dickens, whose brother Alfred was a sanitary inspector, and Andrew Mearns, had depicted workhouses in shocking detail to prick the conscience of the Victorian middle classes. By the Edwardian era, as we show in chapter nine, workhouses had become less terrifying places than their 19th-century predecessors, but their prison-like regimes still imposed fear and a sense of stigma, upon their inmates.

The twists and turns of Liberal governments and prime ministers, from 1906 to 1914, are well-recorded. This book is concerned with another, more intimate, history – how pieces of national legislation, often tortuously evolved, were played out in the council chamber and how they were implemented by sanitary inspectors and other public officials – individuals who are rarely credited for their labours. Their work has had a remarkable cumulative effect. In 1900, more than half of all deaths occurred to people below the age of 45, with infectious disease the main cause; in 2009, this had reduced to 4.4 per cent.

It is common to see the Edwardian period as a golden era – a time of peace, prosperity and the innocent pleasures of horse racing, motoring and country-house weekends. But it is important to remember the inequality of British society – one per cent of the population held 70 per cent of the wealth – and, also, how dangerous work was in manual occupations.

Rates of injury and death in the Edwardian workplace were horrifying by modern standards. In 1908, 1,300 men were killed in accidents in mines and quarries and 148,000 were seriously injured; 432 railway men were killed at work. Every year, on average, one miner in 600 would be killed and one in six seriously injured. Working-class conscripts and volunteers facing the grim horrors of the First World War would have been all too familiar with seeing their colleagues killed and maimed.

When it comes to social welfare, moral questions are frequently entwined within political debates. In the Edwardian period, society's opinion formers were poised between two sets of moral assumptions. These were exemplified by the majority and minority reports of the Royal Commission on the Poor Laws and the Relief of Distress (see chapters two and nine). One set of views harked back to the prevailing Victorian notion that poverty should be seen as a failure of character or ignorance, and that hard work and moral education would provide better escape routes for the poor than undiscriminating public welfare; another stressed universal, state-provided services and benefits. The second approach would rise to prominence as the 20th-century progressed. It would find expression, ultimately, in the bundle of services and benefits that came to be called the welfare state, based on the comprehensive schema of the Beveridge Report of 1942 and including the National Health Service. William Beveridge, a Liberal, author of the report, had helped to draw up the National Insurance Act of 1911. He provides an interesting link between the Edwardian and post-World War Two periods.

As Britain enters an era of economic turbulence, the welfare state model, trimmed and adapted by the neo-liberalism of the 1980s and 1990s, is in retreat. Edwardian preoccupations with the role of central and local government versus charity and mutual-aid organisations in social provision have returned. According to the discourse of the "big society", the state is over-sized; meanwhile, debates on welfare have a flavour of Edwardian discussions on the "deserving" and "undeserving" poor. Is it merely a coincidence that the government is headed by an old-Etonian and that Downton Abbey, an Edwardian costume drama, is our most popular Sunday night television viewing?

Sanitary Inspectors were rarely political creatures, except at their annual dinners, when drink was consumed and spirits ran high (see chapter one). They were, and their successors still are, public servants rather than political theorists. But there are clearly political dimensions to their work. Getting rid of slums is one thing, but why do people live in poor housing and eat poor diets? Such questions are bound to be asked.

This book focuses on how public health policy and practice have been pursued by collective effort, particularly through democratically-elected and accountable local government. To the modern counterparts of the Edwardian sanitary inspectors, it is respectfully dedicated.

*William Hatchett*

*Note: If most of the examples and case studies in this book relate to England, this merely reflects the fact that the authors had most access to English source material. No slight is intended to Wales, Scotland and Northern Ireland, the conditions, professional traditions and legislation of which mirrored, but did not always exactly follow, those in England.*

*References to money use the pre-decimal system of shillings and pence: for example, 3s and 6d (a shilling is the equivalent of 5 pence). Weights and measures refer to imperial rather then metric units.*

# CHAPTER 1

# The Public Health Traditions

*No work calls for higher qualifications than that of the public
health service; no work makes greater demands upon the health
and intelligence of the worker, but in no other department of work
are there greater opportunities of doing real, permanent good, and
the interest is immense.*

*Edith L. Maynard, Women in the Public Health Service, 1915*

On a misty, drizzly night in January, 1910, a group of men
in thick coats with mud on their boots gathered in the
New Gaiety Restaurant, in the Strand, for an important
event in their calendar. It was an occasion that the history
books have hitherto overlooked – the annual dinner of the Sanitary
Inspectors' Association. As a contemporary account in their journal
relates, they had come far – from the Vale of Rhondda, smokeless
Sheffield, distant Durham and the remote parts of Norfolk.

The sanitary inspectors were summoned by the booming voice of
a majordomo into the opulent Adam Chamber and the presence of
their president – the magnificently whiskered Sir James Crichton-
Browne. He was a man of stature – a Fellow of the Royal Society
and a world authority on neuroscience and psychiatric disorders.
An announcement was made – dinner is served. With a sense of
excitement and anticipation, the sanitary inspectors filed to their
appointed places.

As well as speeches and toasts, the dinner included charming
musical interludes – a song from the Gondoliers and Miss Lillie
Selden on her mandolin. There was even a humorous sketch, "The
Honeysuckle and the Bee", performed by Charles Osborne.

The sanitary inspectors must have felt, as they laughed and rapped
on tables with their cutlery, their eyes shining, that they had come
a long way. Their predecessors, inspectors of nuisances, had been
appointed as a direct result of the Public Health Act of 1848. Their
professional association was incorporated in 1883. A year later, Sir
Edwin Chadwick, aged 84, and a leading light of Victorian sanitary
reform, had consented to be their president.

The association's 27th annual dinner, in 1910, was its largest and grandest so far. As well as Crichton-Browne, it attracted other eminent figures – an earl, an archdeacon, an MP, two lord mayors, a judge and senior officials from the Local Government Board and the Home Office.

The association now had 1,350 members in England and Wales, organised into a network of branches. It had instituted its own professional examinations, as an alternative to those provided by the Sanitary Institute (later the Royal Society of Health). Its members, who worked for local authorities, were beginning to achieve security of tenure, rather than annual appointment, and pensions.

As the sanitary inspectors sat down for their dinner, the clamour for votes for women was growing stronger – in 1910, the campaign which had already seen mass demonstrations, was to enter a more militant phase. Reflecting the growing role of women in public life, the male association was shadowed by a Women's Sanitary Inspectors' Association (see chapter four).

Reform was in the air – socialism even. At the twilight of the 19th-century, the mood for change had even affected the Conservatives. Pricked into action by the Liberals, they had set up elected county councils, based on a universal male franchise, and the London County Council. In its early years, the LCC was dominated by Progressives, including the popular Battersea engineer, John Burns, who would go on to take on a prominent role in central government as president of the Local Government Board (see chapter two). The LCC successfully pushed for the introduction of council housing, creating blocks and then estates all over the capital, a model adopted by other British cities.

This housing was not for the poorest (and, in some cases, displaced them to other places): it was designed for those on secure artisans' incomes. But it was certainly a massive improvement on the congested slums of the Victorian era and made a vast contribution to the health and visual amenity of the capital. Much – indeed most – LCC housing survives, including beautiful "arts and crafts" estates in Tottenham and Tooting and the 1930s, balcony-access blocks that pepper inner-London. This housing stock is still fulfilling a valuable public health role.

Conservative Prime Minister from 1895 to 1902, the Marquess of

Salisbury was to observe of the LCC, with regret, for he had been a prime mover in its foundation:"It is the place where collectivist and socialistic experiments are tried. It is the place where a new revolutionary spirit finds its instruments and collects its arms."

Since 1906, Liberal governments, led by Sir Henry Campbell-Bannerman and Herbert Asquith, had pushed through audacious reforms – health visiting, free school meals (not mandatory), school medical inspections, old-age pensions, state health insurance, planning powers for councils and beefed-up slum housing legislation.

In January, 1910, Asquith was in the middle of a "titanic struggle" as The Sanitary Journal described it, to pass his People's Budget, increasing taxation, including a controversial "super tax" for those on the astonishing income of more than £3,000 a year. The House of Lords would give way to Asquith's budget in April; its power to veto bills would be permanently curtailed the following year.

No wonder the sanitary inspectors were jubilant on that night in London – the wind was in their sails. And the presence of their president, Sir James Crichton-Browne, a polymath and a doyen of the scientific establishment, must have added glamour and a sense of anticipation to their evening.

He was no snob or stuffed shirt – why else would he have lent his illustrious name to their association? In an age of public meetings, which valued oratory highly, he was an excellent and entertaining speaker, adopting a "sophisticated vernacular" recalling his Dumfries childhood.

An outspoken man, Crichton-Browne was a scathing opponent of the "fad" of vegetarianism and the florid claims of table rappers and other psychic investigators. He regarded the coming of the motor car, which had brought swirling clouds of dust in its wake, as a health menace and argued for the wider adoption of balloon travel. He was no teetotaller, saying that: "No writer has done much without alcohol."

He also flirted with eugenics – the science of scientific breeding – but, in 1910, this was not particularly controversial (see chapter eight); so did George Bernard Shaw, H.G. Wells, many other Fabians and socialists, and the President of the Board of Trade, Winston Churchill.

Born in 1840, in Edinburgh, to a noted scientific family, he had spent his childhood in the Crichton Royal asylum in Dumfries, where his father was superintendent, and studied medicine at Edinburgh University, completing his thesis, with a characteristic touch of the surreal, on hallucinations. The lunatic asylum was to become his milieu – in 1866, he was appointed medical director of the West Riding Asylum, in Wakefield. Here, he established a neurological research laboratory (there were plenty of brains to dissect), co-founded the world's first journal devoted to neuroscience, Brain, and wrote reports and papers that are regarded as classics of medical psychology. In 1875, he became the Lord Chancellor's Visitor in Lunacy.

If some of Crichton-Browne's views were eccentric, or odd, others were quite rational. A liberal man, he favoured the wider use of outdoor regimes for sufferers from tuberculosis, more humane treatment for those with sexually-transmitted diseases, better housing for the poor and restrictions on the use of corporal punishment.

His presidency of the Sanitary Inspectors' Association, which ran from 1902 to 1921, is often overlooked in his list of honours and appointments, but he filled the role conscientiously. And the sanitary inspectors took him to their hearts.

He was certainly on good form on that night, on the 5th January, 1910, in the New Gaiety. With great panache, Crichton-Browne proposed the loyal toast. Edward VII, a heavy smoker and enthusiastic epicurean, was to die, prematurely, only four months after the dinner. The king, he said, is, "the pivot round which our mighty Empire revolves; beloved by all his subjects, revered by those who are beyond the pale, combining world-wide sagacity with fine human sympathy".

And the sanitary inspectors? Well, no less important, they are "part of the national machinery for the maintenance and improvement of the health of the people". "Fifty years ago," Crichton-Browne told his audience, "the national death rate was close on 22 per thousand living… and what was it for 1908? Why, only 14.7. That represents a gigantic saving of human life and of human suffering and capacity."

He recalls that, when he left university, the term microbe had not yet been coined. He had not attended a single lecture on hygiene, or sanitation, or dietetics. However, things have moved on: "Today there is no department of medical science more enlightened, more exact and more practical than that of preventive medicine."

Squaring up to his audience, he says (to ironic cheers): "There was a time when they [sanitary inspectors] were not up to the mark. They were recruited from the ranks of broken-down tradesmen and they knew about as much about sanitation as they did about Sanskrit." But that has changed and now, " I would say that there is no body of men in the country who are doing more useful work, no body of men more determined to raise the status of their calling and improve their qualifications and efficiency, no body of men more cheerful and undaunted."

He continues: "They see more than other men, except the police and the more devoted of the clergy, the dark and gruesome side of life, of the clotted masses of squalor and misery that clog our civilisation and yet they do not commit suicide or sink into melancholy or misanthropy, but push on with their work, undismayed, full of hope, because they believe in it and witness its beneficial effect."

Their inspection duties, he explains, are multifarious – not least, smoke control and preventing food adulteration and contamination (milk, he observes, is often tainted with tuberculosis and illegally watered down). He notes: "The sanitary inspector who was asked what a sanitary inspector inspects replied 'everything'."

How did the sanitary inspectors' role come about? To answer this question, we must turn to the imposing figure of Sir Edwin Chadwick. The facts of his life are well-recorded. He was born in Longsight, in Manchester, in 1800, to a journalist father, privately educated in London from 1810, trained as a lawyer and called to the bar at the Inner Temple. Always interested in writing, he produced articles for the Morning Herald and, like Dickens, for the Westminster Review. From 1829, he served as secretary to the utilitarian philosopher, Jeremy Bentham. Bentham died three years later, leaving Chadwick a legacy.

In 1832, Chadwick accepted the post that was to shape the rest of his life – assistant commissioner to the Commission of Enquiry on the Poor Laws. Because of his diligence and efficiency he was soon promoted, to commissioner. Some of the adjectives applied to Chadwick are as follows – dogmatic, arrogant, over-confident, tactless, impatient, humourless, doctrinal and priggish. For the establishment, whose mouthpiece was The Times, he came to epitomise a high-handed and doctrinaire approach that was attempting to fetter British individualism. An editorial in the newspaper, in 1854, noted: "We prefer to take our chance with cholera and the rest than be bullied into health." Having helped to draft the 1834 Poor Law Amendment Act, Chadwick became secretary to the new Poor Law Commission. Disagreements began to set in, contributing to the commission breaking up and being replaced by a new board in 1847.

It was an age of Royal Commissions, boards and enquiries, and Chadwick had a role in many of them. He played an important part in the introduction of birth and death registration in 1836; in the evolution of London's sewers (he was a commissioner on London's Metropolitan Commission of Sewers from 1848 to 1849); child and adult labour protection, leading to the 1847 Ten-Hour Act; preventive policing; the health of soldiers in the Crimean War; and recruitment to the civil service.

But he is known, primarily, as a sanitary reformer. With his friend the physician, Thomas Southwood Smith (the man who carried out a public dissection of the corpse of Jeremy Bentham), Chadwick embarked upon examination of sanitary issues and their relationship with disease, initially in the East End of London and then on a larger scale.

He produced, in 1842, at his own expense, an Enquiry into the Labouring Population of Great Britain. This led to a Royal Commission on the Health of Towns, which, in turn, contributed to the Public Health Act of 1848. This important act set up a national General Board of Health (Chadwick was one the board's three commissioners), and introduced local boards, responsible for sewerage, water supply, inspecting slaughterhouses and burial grounds.

Each board employed a medical officer, a surveyor (usually an engineer) and an inspector of nuisance. It was because of Chadwick that the boards' prime purpose was removing filth, and included a medical officer, also a feature of Poor Law unions. Residents could petition for them, or they could be created, automatically, where death rates were high. By 1864, more than 400 towns had taken up the powers.

Britain's first full-time inspector of nuisances was Thomas Fresh, in Liverpool. His post was created through private legislation a year before the 1848 Public Health Act. Fresh managed 13 staff – two assistant inspectors, a chief clerk, two midden clerks, a report clerk, a notice and cellar clerk, four cellar officers (cellar dwellings were common in Liverpool), and two general officers who checked general conditions and measured the dimensions of lodging houses for the medical officer. His salary, £170, was relatively generous. The medical officer, Dr William Henry Duncan, earned £750, the city surveyor £700 and the town clerk a vertiginous £2,000.

Inspectors of nuisance evolved, effectively, as the "eyes and ears" of the medical officer. Speaking in 1892, Sir Benjamin Ward Richardson, president of the Sanitary Inspectors' Association, explained: "The medical officer of health wanted someone who would not be afraid to inspect any nuisance or go into any place where there was fever or other contagious disorders. It was necessary that he should be a… respectable man, and had to be, to some extent, presentable in private houses. His duties were laborious, his salary contemptible."

With each decade, the role of the inspector evolved in terms of its functions and the educational and personal qualities required of the post-holder. In The Sanitary Journal of October, 1910, Francis Vacher, president of the Sanitary Inspectors' Association's North-Western Centre, gives us the Edwardian ideal. The inspector, he argues, should be healthy and fit and schooled to at least the age of 14. A working knowledge of many topics is required – nuisances, food inspection, infectious disease, disinfection, refuse destruction and the purification of sewage. Inspectors need to be practised in book keeping, report writing, typewriting and drawing.

Lady inspectors, says Vacher somewhat patronisingly, have found valuable niches in inspecting female lodging houses and factories employing women, as well as sick nursing and health visiting; he suggests, however, that they should not be used for food duties or the inspection of scavengers and holds that: "Where a local authority is only able to appoint one sanitary inspector, this of course should be a man." The inspector, he proposes, should have a hobby. He suggests country walks, sketching, photography or fishing – or how about golf or football? A hobby that "keeps a man indoors", such as reading or writing, is not recommended.

A photograph taken in 1910 of members of the Sanitary Inspectors' Association's Great Council tells us an eloquent story. These are substantial men with frock coats, wing collars and bowler hats. If not in the upper echelons of society, they are representatives of its managerial classes. So were the hardy female pioneers (see chapter four) who had entered this sphere of work. *Women in the Public Health Service*, by Edith Maynard, formerly chief woman sanitary inspector of Leeds, published in 1915, focuses on infant work and health visiting, which had become female specialisms.

Respectable: General Council and NE Centre Officers, 1910

Like John Ruskin or Octavia Hill (see chapter five), she adopts the tone of one who is looking down on the poor from a higher social position: "Ignorance, poverty, laziness and sometimes ill-health on the part of the mother are the principal opposing factors. To meet the first the official must possess good powers, both of clear explanation and persuasion."

But let us return to Edwin Chadwick. We must note here that he was a miasmist. He held strongly, at least at the beginning of his career in public health, that diseases were produced by an invisible gas, or miasma, generated, in a process known as pythogenesis, by decaying matter. By this reasoning, if waste – decaying carcases, ordure on the streets, filthy water – was efficiently removed, there would be no cholera, tuberculosis or smallpox. In the days of the cesspit and outdoor privy, of inner-city husbandry and toxic industries, when all filth was dumped into the nearest river, it was a good idea to clean up towns and cities, just as it was to treat victims of cholera, smallpox and typhoid in isolation hospitals, a measure initially based on practical observation rather than science. But, in some cases, Chadwick's zeal for cleanliness had unintended consequences. For example, as a London sewer commissioner in the 1840s, he ordered storm drains containing human waste to be flushed into the Thames, from which drinking water was extracted. This must have contributed to the incidence of cholera.

His spell, after the Public Health Act of 1848, as a commissioner on the General Board of Health ended, typically, in acrimony. His bluntness and unwillingness to compromise had upset many. He was forced into retirement in 1854, when the board was broken up. Poor Law Commissioners Lord Shaftesbury and Thomas Southwood Smith were also summarily dispensed with. Chadwick now lobbied on sanitary matters. He stood, unsuccessfully for Parliament in 1867. In 1883, as we have noted, he became the first president of the Sanitary Inspectors' Association. He was not knighted until 1890, the year that he died.

In 1855, the powers of the former General Board of Health were transferred to the Privy Council and a new man was brought in to run it. Sir John Simon, a well-known London physician, was the opposite to Chadwick – tactful, diplomatic, open-minded and au fait with the latest scientific discoveries. In his new role of Chief Medical Officer (a post that continues to this day), Simon was the first public official to advise central government on matters relating to health. Simon had previously served as London's first medical officer after the 1848 Public Health Act. It was the year of a large cholera epidemic. With skill and application, he had designed a job for which there was no template – collecting mortality statistics and advising on sanitary measures. His annual reports are still referred to as models of their kind.

In 1858, Simon was influential in the passing of the Medical Act, establishing the General Medical Council, which regulated doctors. A Royal Sanitary Commission in 1868 led to the expansion of local health boards, now to be called sanitary authorities (and later to become urban and rural districts). In 1871, the Local Government Board was set up to run local government and to take over the functions of the former Poor Law Board. Simon became its senior medical officer. But this new civil servant's role did not suit him. He felt that the medical aspects of the new organisation were not given enough priority, as opposed to the merely administrative tasks of running the country's workhouses. The poor law inspectors who worked for him, for example, had no medical qualifications.

He resigned in 1876, to devote his time, like Chadwick, to a variety of public health-related tasks, including writing a substantial volume called English Sanitary Institutions, which was published in 1897. It can be found in the CIEH library. Always diplomatic, after devoting many pages to his faults, Simon writes flatteringly of Chadwick: "How permanently important has been the momentum which State-Medicine received from the vigour and substantial conclusiveness of [his] advocacy."

While his writing has the moralising tone of the Victorian era, Simon's working methods were scientific and deductive – devise a hypothesis and collect evidence to test it – as opposed to Chadwick's inductive approach, working from the specific to the general. In the middle of the century, a pioneer epidemiologist, Dr John Snow, had demonstrated a correlation between polluted drinking water and cholera, particularly in connection with the 1854 Broad Street outbreak in Soho. And, from the 1860s, the discoveries of Louis Pasteur and Robert Koch led to what would become known as germ theory. It was becoming clear that diseases were causes by physical agencies that could be viewed through a microscope, rather than pythogenesis, as held by the miasmists. Those who, like Simon, subscribed to the new microbial theory were known as contagionists.

As the century came to a close, the miasmist and contagionist traditions underpinned two branches of public health – there was a medical branch, favouring epidemiology and programmes of education and vaccination, and a sanitary branch, concentrating on improving the physical environment. Both were equally important, but their practitioners tended to distrust each other, the sanitarians with a sense of grievance because of their lower salaries and social status than the medics. The sanitarians tended to view themselves as multi-skilled, knowledgeable in many practical disciplines, and the law, and under-valued.

They had substantial evidence of success on their side. For example, they could point with pride to Joseph Bazalgette's astonishing system of London sewers, begun in 1858 – 82 miles of trunk sewers, 1,100 miles of branch sewers, four pumping stations and two major treatment works. This ambitious undertaking, it is estimated, increased average life expectancy in Victorian London by 20 years.

There must have been delegates at the Sanitary Inspectors' Association annual dinner in 1910 whose views were closer to those of the recently-deceased Chadwick (happily his body unlike that of his philosophical mentor, Bentham, was not stuffed and put on public display) than to those of Simon. Some of them would still have been nostalgic for the old certainties of the 1850s. Each decade since then had brought new wonders – microbes, the electric telegraph, the typewriter, the telephone, the motor car – but the old miasmist ideas and the terms associated with them, such as zymotic disease, took a long time to die out.

Sir James Crichton-Browne, the eloquent after-dinner speaker, was a healing figure. He reassured his audience that they were needed, and valuable, not "broken down tradesmen". He understood that they sat on the shoulders of two great knights, Chadwick and Simon; that there were two principal causes of disease, pathogens and filth; and that sanitary inspectors, cogs in the national machinery, were well-qualified to sort them out.

His witty speech, the wine, the brandy and the conviviality of the evening must have made the inspectors go back to the Rhondda, Sheffield, Durham and Norfolk feeling content, despite the mud and the cold, buoyed up and ready for the rigours and challenges of the year ahead. Soon, they would be able to read about the evening, and see the flashlight photograph, reproduced in their monthly journal.

*William Hatchett*

## CHAPTER 2

# Poverty

*Our main conclusions, drawn from the facts reported and endorsed*
*by the Royal Commission… were that the chief industrial*
*causes of pauperism were as follows: first, casual and irregular*
*employment. Second, bad housing. Third, unhealthy trades and*
*insanitary, injurious and exhausting conditions of employment.*
*Fourth, low wages, that is, earnings habitually below what is*
*required for healthy subsistence.*
        *Rose E. Squire, Thirty Years in the Public Service, 1927*

The same things caused illness in Edwardian Britain as today – exposure to germs, being bitten by things, pollution, cold, excessive heat, damp, diet, contaminated food or water, accidents, occupation, and inheritance. All but inheritance and workplaces covered by national inspectorates were in the province of the sanitary inspector.

Bacteria and viruses had been discovered and the biochemical actions of poisons and toxins on the human body were well understood. It was known that some debilitating conditions were hereditary, giving an underpinning to the surprisingly numerous advocates of eugenics (see chapter eight). This was a theory designed to discourage or prevent people deemed the weakest from reproducing, as if human beings were prize cattle or sheep.

Poverty as a contributor to mortality had been comprehensively demonstrated: for example, by the Royal Commissions and Parliamentary blue books that Karl Marx pored over in the British Library in the 1850s, and in the typologies and maps of Henry Mayhew's three-volume London Labour and the London Poor, published in 1851. In fact, the poor had been endlessly examined, categorised and pinned by the energetic Victorians, like the moths and butterflies in one of their natural history museums.

There was extremely unequal income distribution in Edwardian Britain. Of the 40 million population, 99 per cent earned £150 a year or less; only 10,000 earned more than £700. At the top were the landed aristocracy not yet scythed down by taxes and the First World

War, and, in descending order, the managerial and white collar class – a male teacher earned from £150 to £200 a year – then servants – a butler earned, on average, £60 a year, a maid £18 – and the skilled and unskilled working class.

Beneath them were paupers and the destitute, often depending on the harsh regime of the workhouse and its infirmaries, or hospitals and, for those who were still vertical, casual wards. Ninety per cent of the population rented their accommodation. For the unemployed or those in irregular work, prospects were bleak. In every town and city, families were crammed cheek by jowl into endlessly sub-divided houses and their damp, festering cellars.

In 1839, Edwin Chadwick, had objected to the term starvation being included by William Farr – the pioneer statistician and epidemiologist – as a cause of death. Farr, an important figure in the history of public health, worked in the General Register office, set up in 1836. Chadwick maintained, with implacable logic, that it should not be possible to starve, thanks to the reformed Poor Law; he never campaigned against poverty, only against filth.

By Edwardian times, great health gains had been made in Britain's cities. There were no more large-scale cholera or typhoid outbreaks, and smallpox and typhus were in retreat; instead, infectious diseases associated with poverty and overcrowding pre-occupied the sanitary inspector – tuberculosis, whooping cough, diphtheria, scarlet fever, measles. These exacted a terrifying toll – at the beginning of the century, infectious disease caused a third of all deaths and 63 per cent of all deaths were premature. In 1900, the wizened specimens who presented themselves at recruiting stations for the Second Boer War shocked the nation – almost half failed to reach the required standard. Concern, and a degree of shame, gave a strong impetus to the Liberals' programme of domestic reforms from 1906.

The Edwardian era was one of evangelism, of public meetings and pamphlets. Thanks to the Forster Education Act of 1870, the working and middle classes had never been so literate. There were now affordable, sometimes illustrated, mass-market newspapers, such as the populist Daily Mail, first published in 1896. In print and in meetings, poverty, a topic that preoccupied the middle classes, was much-debated.

Then, as now, there were many ways to look at poverty, each

with its advocates. The categories were not mutually exclusive and sometimes overlapped. Broadly, there was the laissez-faire approach (do nothing), self-interest (do something, or the poor will kill us), religious (they need saving), moral (teach them self-improvement and piety) utilitarian (apply logic), socially democratic (improve pay, widen the franchise) and revolutionary (appropriate power for the dispossessed). Each had its advocates, in a melting pot of ideas.

It was held by some that too much charity or state aid were bad things – they would only weaken their recipients and encourage dependence. Many people, especially those who lived comfortably, were disposed to blame the poor, with their tendency to drink excessively and to breed immoderately, for their plight. Theories were also abroad that Britain was over-populated or that her racial "stock" was deteriorating; that there were too many imbeciles and their ilk dependent upon rate-based assistance, that too many of the hale and hearty were going to the colonies, leaving a sickly residuum. Winston Churchill's views (which are discussed in chapter eight) must have been common amongst a segment of the middle and upper classes – he was unselfconsciously in favour of the confinement, segregation and sterilisation of the "feeble-minded".

John Simon, in his English Sanitary Institutions of 1897, issues a stern warning against the recruits into "loafer life" – the able-bodied who flagrantly beg or claim Poor Law relief. He says: "Their idleness is so wilful an offence against the community as to deserve treatment of a penal character." He opines that the state ought to intervene against "the hereditary continuance of pauperism" and have powers to remove children from irresponsible parents.

Charities, he asserts, do not discriminate enough between genuine need and "sham poverty" or "fraudulent mendacity"; they should promote "proper habits of prudence" and leave those in most need to poor law relief. A proposal to provide free or cheap meals to elementary school children raises his hackles. He argues that such a measure would be destructive of family life, exonerating parents from "the duty of feeding their children". Simon, whose stern moral tone is more Victorian than Edwardian, is concerned that there are too many charities in London, including hospitals providing "gratuitous medical treatment".

Others were preoccupied with determining the scale of the

problem. Charles Booth and Benjamin Seebohm Rowntree (who was generally known by his second name) shared similar backgrounds and motivations. Charles Booth was an unlikely social researcher. The heir of a successful Liverpool shipping company, rather than lounging on the Riviera, he decided to devote his time to researching the causes of poverty. Booth's The Life and Labour of the People of London was published in two volumes in 1891. By 1902, it had expanded to 17 volumes. Combining description with statistical analysis, it was the Edwardian equivalent of Mayhew's compendious London Labour and the London Poor.

Booth and his researchers, including his cousin, Beatrice Webb, painstakingly drew up an economic map of London, colour-coded, street-by-street. They adopted eight categories from A to H. Black was the colour used for the lowest class streets ("vicious, semi-criminal"); dark and light blue for the very poor and those in chronic want; pink for the "fairly comfortable"; red for the middle class, and so on. Booth popularised the concept of a poverty line, which he set at 21s a week, or £55 a year, for an average family. He maintained from his research, shockingly, that almost a third of London's population, who lived in classes A to C, were beneath it.

Booth was not merely a theoretician: he lodged with poor families in the East End, in order to get to know them. He did not seek to identify cures for poverty; rather he saw his work as devising scientific ways to measure it, for which he was honoured by the Royal Society and the Royal Statistical Society. His personal politics wavered. He was in favour of old-age pensions (if only to prevent socialist revolution) but opposed to the political influence of trades unions on the Liberal party. In later life, he transferred his support from the Liberals to the Conservatives. Booth is regarded as a pioneer sociologist and statistician and was made a fellow of the Royal Society in 1882 for "having applied scientific methods to social investigation" but his reflections are not immune from what, today, we would call moralising. He says in Life and Labour: "I fear that the bulk of those whose earnings are irregular are wanting in prudence. Provident thrift, which lays by for tomorrow, is not a very hardy plant in England, and needs the regular payment of weekly wages to take root freely."

His findings were influential on the work of Seebohm Rowntree, who conducted a study of 12,000 families, in York, in 1899. Rowntree also came from a wealthy background – his father Joseph, was the Quaker founder of the Rowntree chocolate company. Rowntree asked experts (nutrition was a science in its infancy – vitamins had not been discovered yet) to determine a minimum healthy diet. He factored in the outgoings needed for rent, household items, light, fuel and clothing, and established, although some disputed his findings, that 28 per cent of York's population lived below the poverty line.

Published in 1901, his Poverty: A Study of Town Life, caused a stir. People knew that there was grinding poverty in the gin and beer-sodden East End and perhaps in Manchester, Birmingham and Liverpool; they hardly associated it with a northern cathedral city.

I f you wish to write about the poor with authority, it helps if you live among them. And, in the Edwardian era, William Booth, social campaigner and founder of the Salvation Army, certainly did. Booth was born in Nottingham in 1829 and was privately educated until his father became bankrupt. He joined the Methodists when he was 15. Five years later, he moved to London, working, initially, in the ungodly environment of a pawnbroker's shop. The Salvation Army grew into a worldwide organisation from the outdoor Christian revival meetings that Booth began with his wife, Catherine, in 1861, in the East End. They were not always popular, particularly because of their antipathy to the consumption of alcohol by the poor. People would abuse them in the streets and small boys would throw stones through the windows of the warehouses where they held their services.

Because of its simple message and vigorous style, William Booth's book, in Darkest England and the Way Out, published in 1890, became an improbable best-seller. Its central conceit was to compare Britain to "uncivilized" Africa, as described by contemporary explorers. The book was probably written, although it was denied by Booth, with the help of his friend, W.T. Stead, editor of the tabloid-style Pall Mall Gazette. In the 1880s, Stead had shocked Britain's breakfast table with sensational accounts of child prostitution and the "white slave trade". He was to drown on the maiden voyage of the Titanic in 1912.

Some of what Stead had described in the Pall Mall Gazette was certainly still prevalent in Edwardian times. Working and professional roles for women were severely restricted, prostitution was endemic and "fallen women" were confined in lunatic asylums and workhouses. Other Victorian preoccupations, "sweated labour" and "house farming", were also still common.

Campaigner: William Booth founder of the Salvation Army

Booth describes: "A population sodden with drink, steeped in vice, eaten up by every social and physical malady... the denizens of darkest England". He points out that many in Britain have identified the problems of poverty and destitution but few have come up with solutions: "There are more scientific books treating of diabetes or gout than dealing with the great social malady." His solutions are not merely based on saving souls and abolishing the demon drink; he proposes farm communities for the urban poor, homes for fallen women and released prisoners, specialised banks, clinics and industrial schools, and even a seaside resort.

The American author, Jack London, provides us with another

contemporary depiction of poverty. He was the author of The People of the Abyss, commissioned by a New York publisher as a study of slum life and published in 1903. London was a socialist with eugenicist tendencies. His Call of the Wild, a social Darwinist parable set in the Klondike, also first published in 1903, was to make him famous.

The People of the Abyss is well-described, compassionate and insightful. Wearing a specially acquired suit of ragged clothes, with a gold sovereign stitched into his vest, London "carries the banner" – that is spends the night on the streets, constantly moved on by policemen. He gives us a first-hand account of the facilities that were available to the able-bodied London pauper in Edwardian times.

One of the chilling things about the book, based on a visit to Britain in August 1902, is the fact that London is one of hundreds, if not thousands, of people tramping the streets of the capital, shuffling miserably between workhouses and soup kitchens. This is welfare on a military or industrial scale – an aspect of Edwardian Britain that we do not normally glimpse. London, as an American, is particularly appalled by the conditions he encounters – the American working-man is far better paid than his British equivalent. In his own country, food is more plentiful and cheaper, even for the hobo.

Workhouse casual wards, or "spikes", were facilities for those who did not require long-term accommodation. It was a rule that those admitted must spend two nights and a day in the workhouse and carry out manual labour. In the Poplar spike, men wearing stinking clothes with rags wrapped around their feet must first have a cold bath. Tobacco and matches are taken away. For supper, they are given six ounces of bread and three-quarters of a pint of skilly (oatmeal and water); they rise at 5.30 am and, after a bread and skilly breakfast, are set to work, picking oakum (old rope) or breaking up stones. Lunch consists of 10 ounces of bread. After another night's accommodation, they must go back onto the street. Applicants can only present themselves at another workhouse at least 10 miles distant, so must spend the whole day walking. How then, London asks, are they supposed to find a job?

He gives us portraits of two vagrants waiting to enter the Whitechapel spike. "In both instances, I found that the smallpox was the cause of their being 'on the doss'... Both [men] had been working when smitten by the disease, and both had emerged from the hospital broke, with the gloomy task of hunting for work. They had come to the spike to rest up after three days and nights on the street... It seems that not only the man who becomes old is punished for his involuntary misfortune but, likewise, the man who is struck by disease."

Another man in the line, Ginger, a porter, had been carrying a heavy box of fish when "something broke" in his back. He is now incapable of heavy work. The pattern of his future life has been set – he will drift between the spike, soup kitchens, doss houses and the street until he dies.

London sleeps in the Whitechapel workhouse, "in a long, narrow room, traversed by two iron rails. Between these rails were stretched not hammocks by pieces of canvas, six feet long and less than two feet wide... [the beds] were six inches apart and about eight inches from the floor... many hours passed before I won sleep...the smell was frightful and sickening, while my imagination broke loose and my skin crept and crawled till I was nearly frantic... grunting, groaning and snoring arose, like the sounds emitted by some sea monster."

Next morning, he must place infected rubbish from the sick wards into sacks at the nearby Whitechapel Infirmary. At eight o'clock in the evening, dinner is served – in the cellar. An "indescribable mess" of the patients' leavings, it is composed of "pieces of bread, chunks of grease and pork fat, burnt skin from the outside of roasted joints and bones".

At the Salvation Army barracks in Blackfriars Road, he waits for two hours, with 700 men, for breakfast. In the "feasting hall" they sit down, "not to meat or bread, but to speech, song and prayer". Breakfast arrives at eleven o'clock in paper parcels – three slices of bread, one with currants in it, a slice of cheese and a mug of "bewitched" water, euphemistically called tea. Some of the famished men have been queuing since five o'clock in the morning for food tickets. They are required to participate in another religious service before they are allowed to leave.

According to London, almost half a million people in the capital live in one-room tenements, a further million are "illegally and viciously housed" and about 40,000 live in common lodging-houses or as "doss-houses". Doss houses had been registered and inspected since 1851 and came under the remit of sanitary inspectors. London says that the larger and municipal facilities, while grim and spartan, have reached an acceptable standard. However, the small, private doss-houses are "an unmitigated horror".

He visits a large doss house not far from Middlesex Street, in Whitechapel. This establishment has a dining room and a smoking room, equipped with billiards tables and draughts boards. Here, "men were sitting around, smoking, reading, and mending their clothes… On the walls were the most preposterous and insulting notices regulating the conduct of the guests, and at ten o'clock the lights were put out, and nothing remained but bed."

He sleeps in a partitioned cubicle or "cabin" for which he has paid 5d in a large dormitory. The room and bedding are clean, but no privacy is possible. "If you care to remain a guest in this poor man's hotel, you must put up with all this, and with prison regulations which impress upon you constantly that you are nobody, with little soul of your own and less to say about it."

London had not meant to research a book about poverty. He had been en-route to South Africa to report conditions after the Boer War for the American Press Association but he was so shocked by what he encountered in Britain that he changed the purpose of his trip. His visit coincided with the coronation of King Edward VII. Standing in Trafalgar Square, he is far more interested in studying the crowds than the procession of priests, soldiers and statesmen that files past. He notices, at once, that the magnificent guardsmen with their steel breastplates are giants compared to the stunted pavement dwellers among whom he is standing. The soldiers and policemen need to be fed on beefsteaks, he observes, so that they can subdue the hungry masses upon whose toil the nation's wealth depends – social Darwinism in action.

Edwardian Britain provided a fertile medium for political organisation and debate. Strands of Conservative and Liberal thought were now complemented by left-wing political organisations. The dissemination of Marxist theories had produced, by the 1880s, Britain's first socialist party, the Social Democratic Federation (which soon split into revolutionary and reforming wings). From the trade union movement, came the Labour Representation Committee, which gained two MPs in 1900 and, in 1906, became the Labour party.

The Fabian Society, which had begun in 1884 as The Fellowship of the New Life to promote socialist ideas, was influential as what, today, we might call a think tank. It was prolific in its production of pamphlets on social and political issues. A Fabian pamphlet in 1894 notes that one in five of London's population is a pauper and that one in eight deaths in London takes place in a workhouse or other poor law institution.

It adds: "No distinction is made between the professional idler and worker who, through accident, sickness or misfortune is thrown onto the rates." Deliberate dishonour, says the pamphlet, is assigned to the old age of the poor. Children, it adds, should not be taught in Poor Law "barrack schools" but in public elementary schools. The practice of placing them out as labourers or errand boys should be abandoned. The pamphlet also calls, prophetically, for state pensions for the aged, health insurance and the reform of the casual ward.

Britain's Empire was now at its peak. Its industries, based on coal and steel, were burgeoning. London was the largest and wealthiest city in the world. But, as Jack London had shown, there was another face to the city – extreme poverty. It was apparent, to most shades of political opinion, that the poor law inherited from the Victorians was not fit for purpose in the 20th century. In any case, the system, with its workhouses, casual wards and dispensaries appeared to be creaking at the seams in the face of huge demand.

It was the Conservatives, under Arthur Balfour, who convened, in 1904, a Royal Commission on the Poor Laws and Relief of Distress. The Liberals inherited the commission when they won unexpectedly, under Sir Henry Campbell Bannerman, a substantial election victory in 1906.

The inquiry was almost unprecedented in its importance, scope and scale. An excellent account of its modus operandi is given by one of its "special investigators", the pioneering female sanitary and factory inspector, Rose Squire (see chapter four).

Appointed because of her "tact and skill", Squire was asked to investigate "the relation of industrial and sanitary conditions to pauperism", joining a team of investigators. She and a colleague, A.D. Steel Maitland, were supported by voluntary helpers and two secretaries. After spending three months in London, they visited

Manchester, Liverpool, Sheffield, Birmingham, Bristol, St Helens, the five pottery towns and Cornwall. They combined a survey of official records with face-to-face interviews. Factories, docks and mines were visited and evidence taken from thousands of paupers. Squire had to use her tact and skill to the full, because women were discouraged from entering male places of work and, in many cases, forbidden from going down mines. She describes plunging down a terrifying, 3,000-foot shaft in a coffin-shaped capsule and walking down tunnels with a candle stuck in a ball of clay attached to her hat: "When our party emerged once more into the light of day we were scarcely recognisable and, to me at least, until I had bathed and donned dry garments, life seemed not worth living!"

Cheerful, indefatigable and industrious, she was well-suited to her role. Writing in her memoir, Thirty Years in the Public Service, she recalls investigating in the slums: "Generally, I chatted and questioned while my companion rapidly took notes. We easily obtained all the information we could desire as it was poured out without reserve... we found that a bowler hat held in the hand of the gentleman visitor afforded a convenient screen for the notebook and moving hand of the scribe, and allowed of the friendly chat with the lady being carried on undisturbed!"

At this time, she notes, there was no compensation for industrial diseases, no national health insurance, no old age pensions, widow's pensions or employment exchanges – they would all evolve over the next two decades. Services catering for tuberculosis (the most common cause of destitution) and for infant and maternal welfare were in their infancy. Drink, she admits, was often resorted to when other forms of hope and relief were absent.

Her work made her angry. She writes: "Honest, hard working, steady men were reduced to destitution by the conditions under which they were employed. I cannot recall without hot indignation and shame the cold fact of excessive hours, miserably inadequate wages, exposure to wet, to heat, to dust, to poisonous materials in the heavy iron and steel trades, in chemical works, in white lead, paint and pottery works, to say nothing of the inhuman system (or lack of system) of casual labour at the docks."

After 12 months, she and Steel Maitland duly delivered their hurriedly assembled report to the Royal Commission. The high-profile body was made up of 18 members of the great and the good. It was chaired by a Conservative politician, Lord George Hamilton.

In the course of their work, the commissioners soon split into two opposing camps. On the one hand, were the traditionalists, whose views harked back to the Victorian era. Epitomised by Helen Bosanquet and Octavia Hill of the influential Charity Organisation Society, they focused on what they perceived as the moral causes of poverty, such as laziness, addiction to drink or lack of ambition. They were largely supportive of the existing poor law, including the deterrent effect of workhouses, and against "outdoor relief". They believed, unapologetically, that the poor should be taught to help themselves – they should not be provided with subsidised services, whether from the state or local government, requiring nothing in return.

Representing a minority view, progressives on the commission clustered around Beatrice Webb. Their views looked forwards rather than backwards, towards the 20th century. Socio-economic causes of poverty were stressed; its amelioration, they believed, should be achieved through universal welfare, free of moral judgment or stigma. The poor law should, at worst, be substantially reformed or, at best, abolished.

There were some areas of agreement, but no reconciliation could be achieved between the two camps. In 1909, the commission delivered majority and minority findings. The report's appendix, running to 36 volumes, provides us with an invaluable record of Edwardian working conditions, including, in volume 16, the tragic Cornish silica miners questioned by Rose Squire, who, forced to breathe in toxic dust, coughed up their lives, forcing their widows and children into the poor house. The Liberal government (as we shall see in chapter nine) did not react explicitly to the divided report. But times were changing: the poor law was, by now, crumbling away by default, through national and local action.

No doubt to the distaste of the Charity Organisation Society, the government had introduced school meals in 1906, and school medical inspections and health visiting for pregnant women in 1907. And some local authorities were energetically radical. At their head was the London County Council. In its early days, the LCC was dominated by Progressives, whose leader was John Burns.

Born to a poor family in Lambeth, Burns set up a branch of the

Social Democratic Federation, rose through the trade union ranks and became an LCC councillor in 1890. He was elected as MP for Battersea in 1892 and, in 1905, made president of the Local Government Board with a place on the Privy Council and in the Cabinet – it was said that someone from such humble origins had never achieved such high office.

At the LCC, Burns and the Progressives campaigned for issues at the cutting edge of public health – better schools, cleaner food, pasteurisation of milk, shorter working hours, slum clearance and healthier housing. From the 1890s, the LCC built London and the country's first council estates.

Burns is strongly associated with the historic Housing and Town Planning Act of 1909. This included the first local authority planning powers. It made it easier for sanitary inspectors to enter slum dwellings and, where necessary, have them pulled down. There was still no exchequer subsidy for council housing. Legislation enabling large-scale council house building would not come until 1919.

Such issues, and the laws associated with them, all find expression in the monthly publication of The Sanitary Inspectors' Association that had begun in 1895, The Sanitary Journal. Contemporary social debates, in some cases odd to us, like discussions of eugenics, bounce around between articles and on the letters pages. The Royal Commission on the Poor Laws is hardly likely to be ignored.

In the January, 1910, Sanitary Journal, shortly after the commission's findings were issued, a female sanitary inspector, Miss M. Carey of Westminster, gives her own observation of workhouses and discusses the contents of the majority and minority reports. She reflects of the workhouse regime: "Women who have come in to be confined are compelled to associate day and night and to work side by side with half-witted imbeciles... in the sick wards of minor workhouses we have seen young children in bed with minor ailments next to women of bad character under treatment for contagious diseases."

However, in one London workhouse, conditions, she argues, are far too comfortable: "Owing to the want of classification among the inmates, a relaxation of discipline intended for the aged has been shown to all classes. There is now a class of people who regard it as a clubhouse in which they put up with a certain amount of inconvenience, in return for pleasant evenings."

She comes to a judiciously balanced conclusion: "If only the suggestions on which the reports agree could be carried out a very substantial reform would be effected." The care of the mentally defective, for example, should be removed from the poor law.

But should sanitary inspectors be dipping their toes into the turbulent waters of political controversy – after all, their job is inspecting premises and dealing with nuisance, dispassionately. They are public servants.

As now, the environmental health profession of 1910 was divided. In a later issue of the journal, its editor, the redoubtable H.H. Spears, chief sanitary inspector for West Bromwich, defends Miss Carey. It is acceptable and even desirable, he asserts, for inspectors to address social issues, including poverty.

He comments: "An inspector is, after all, a citizen and we think discussion should not be tabooed on sociological and economic factors that so intimately affect public health progress… we hold very strongly that an inspector's mental horizon should not be bounded by the perimeter of a drainpipe."

*William Hatchett*

CHAPTER 3

# CHAPTER 3
# Mills and Maladies

*One infant that died at the age of ten months and commenced life*
*on humanised milk, was afterwards fed on Marshall's Malted*
*Food, Scott's Emulsion and brandy and cream and, towards its*
*end, veal and tea. Such deplorable ignorance in infant feeding calls*
*for some action on the part of the municipality.*

*Report on the Health of Bradford*
*from the Medical Officer of Health, 1901*

Public health problems were far from over at the beginning of the Edwardian period. The history of the public health profession at this time shows continued but slow progress, mainly through the regulation of various trades, whether that be shopkeeper, mill owner, landlord or midwife. One way to show this is through the work of a particular sanitary department. Although acts of Parliament covered the whole country, it was the work of individual council officers that made the difference. Local authorities could enforce an act with greater or lesser enthusiasm. They could choose to bring in by-laws or not bother. Staff could be appointed to work on a problem or they could be taken off it. There was plenty to do and resources were few.

Bradford was a mill town in the north of England and people from all over the country had been flocking to work in its dark satanic mills since the turn of the previous century. Mill owners (with the possible exception of a Titus Salt who built the village of Saltaire, a model of teetotal philanthropy) were not overly concerned with the welfare of their workers, either in the mills or when they were at home. The canal basin was so polluted that little boys used to set fire to the methane being given off. Near it, workmen "found their silver pocket watches turned black due to the sulphuretted contamination in the air".

Sanitary reformers on their tours of the new industrial cities had also visited and were not impressed. In a report from 1837, a James Smith, of Deanston, said of Bradford: "I am obliged to pronounce it the most filthy town I visited." In 1849, however, another reformer, an Angus Reach, observed: "Smith only said that because he never went to Halifax."

Bradford's health committee met every fortnight and was so important it was chaired by the Lord Mayor himself. It had been presented with an annual report from the council's public health and nuisance department since the middle of the 19th century. During the Edwardian era, Bradford operated a broad programme of inspections and sampling. This was covered by a sub-committee, the remit of which covered public urinals, privy accommodation, common lodging houses, smoke nuisances, general nuisances, cow sheds, slaughterhouses, cellar dwellings and matters arising under the Shop Hours Act. It is safe to assume that its meeting would be somewhat lengthy.

Each year, the first part of the health report listed the incidence and death rate from a number of diseases. Anthrax was known as "wool sorters' disease" because it was so common in the mills. The annual number of cases and deaths varied. In the early years, it was comparatively safe for the wool sorters: three deaths in 1901 and one in 1902. By 1905, there were 20 cases, with a 50 per cent death rate. The annual report of 1910 stated that: "Most of the infected persons were employed in the sorting of wools known to be dangerous." The differences in death rates reflected the different places where the wool was obtained most cheaply.

The medical officer of health noted in his report for 1905 that this year's killer wool had come from Persia. It seems a little strange that this "dangerous wool" was just a fact you had to accept. The reason Persian wool proved so bad was that the spores were breathed in, causing "Internal Anthrax", as opposed to the slightly less dangerous "External Anthrax or Malignant Pustule", as it was tastefully known. The occupations at risk for the wool workers were "carders, combers, sorters, washers, jobbers and pullers". The next year, there were fewer cases (11) and only four deaths. One, however, was a butcher infected while slaughtering an ox.

In 1904, smallpox was re-introduced into the city, firstly by a navvy, recently working in Harrogate, staying in a common lodging house. There were 130 people in the lodging house and they all refused the offer of vaccination. Another case was a cattle drover (smallpox seems to have been an occupational hazard). This man caught the disease while on board a Canadian cattle ship. Smallpox was mainly associated with vagrancy, however, and a conference was held on that subject in London that year. The other problem with smallpox was that people hoped it was only chicken pox and that it would go away by itself. Often, other people in the house would catch the disease before the original victim died or obtained the correct diagnosis.

School attendance was not compulsory under five. But schools were given a government grant if they taught children between three and five, so many teachers tried to entice younger children into their schools to get this money. In 1906, the health report noted: "In many cases, too, parents are glad to get rid of their responsibility."

This was considered a bad thing; at that age children were most susceptible to measles and were catching it at school. "If school authorities stopped these (young ones) going to school there would be a smaller mortality from measles (152 deaths that year) and whooping cough (54), less defective eye sight and more room… for older pupils."

In line: mill workers in 1910 outside a grocery shop in Seymour Street

The health department had an ambulance section during the whole of the Edwardian period. The report for each year invariably stated: "The ambulance equipment consists of two men, two horses and two ambulances," which seems about the right numbers. The men's job was to ferry infectious people to hospital. In 1907, for example, they moved 1,041 cases: about two per day each, if they didn't work weekends.

The consolidating Factory and Workshop Act was introduced in 1901. Sanitary facilities in factories and overcrowding in workshops were the main focus, with requirements for ventilation where gases or fumes were injurious to workers a close second. Underground bake houses in particular were "of much interest to health officers". They were often damp, ill-kempt places, insanitary and dirty; they may also have contained beds or had toilets leading straight into them, and could be closed. Dirty bake houses needed cleaning and whitewashing. The chief inspector at the time saw a problem with this new legislation, as it allowed appeals to the magistrates' court against his department closing insanitary or substandard bake houses. This was an affront to his dignity as he was allowed to decide, unencumbered, on "much more weighty matters". Due to the need for improved sanitary facilities (it is difficult to imagine the state of some of the places that would be met by the inspectors), an order was sought from Parliament to further regulate the situation. Thirty-six bake houses were closed in 1902 and another 36 improved, with one offender prosecuted.

Two years later, the chief inspector's worries proved correct. The prosecution of an insanitary bake house failed, whereupon the council appealed to the High Court. The Yorkshire Daily Observer reported the case in July 1904. The question was whether an old bake house could continue to operate below legal standards, if the legislation was introduced after it commenced in business. After a brief discussion, the Lord Chief Justice said that: "It is apparent that (the bakehouse) cannot be used without a certificate." The council's counsel, a Mr Danckwerts KC, replied, somewhat cheekily: "That would strike the average mind, but it did not strike the mind of the learned magistrate." The Lord Chief Justice allowed the appeal with costs.

The act increased provision for outworkers. Outworking (making things in your own house) was a major problem in Bradford and had been since the time of the notorious wool-combers' dwellings. These were overcrowded, insanitary rooms where the fumes from the charcoal burners (necessary to warm and soften the raw wool to make disentangling it easier) had led to many deaths the previous century. New provisions made it illegal to produce "wearing apparel on premises infected with scarlet fever or smallpox". The inspectors also made visits under the Shop Hours Act. Problems they found included children who worked more than 74 hours a week, or in a shop and, on the same day, in a factory. In 1903, 2,629 visits were made to shops with 10 failing the provision on hours of employment of young persons.

The Shop Seats Act 1899 required shops to provide one seat for every three female assistants. Inspectors made sure the provisions were adhered to with an enthusiastic 194 inspections in 1901. By 1911, 279 shops were visited. Only one had not provided seats for lady shop workers and was served with a warning notice. The owners rushed out and got one immediately.

A form of partnership working happened between the Factory Inspectorate and the local authority in those days. In 1904, 116 complaints were notified to the factory inspectors where officers had noted that abstracts of the Factory and Workshop Act were not being displayed. When problems with sanitary accommodation were found during factory safety inspections, the factory inspector wrote to the town clerk and workshop and sanitary inspectors went to deal with the problem. In 1911, 60 such complaints were made.

The Employment of Children Act 1903 further limited hours of work and the lifting of heavy weights or anything injurious to the life, limb or education of a child. In that year, 1,142 children under the age of 14 were found employed after nine in the evening or before six in the morning. One boy, who was of "weak intellect and delicate constitution", was "employed long hours as a carrier's assistant, "in all weathers". This was considered to injure both him and his education; the family and employer were warned and he was quickly out of a job. By 1906, 215 children were found who were employed for the whole of Saturday, 13 working under the age of 11, 103 employed mornings and evenings, 110 during school meal hours, and two before 6 am. The meals offence is interestingly. Presumably, people were so desperate that as soon as the school bell was rung for lunch, children were put to work until dinnertime was over.

The act defined 315 separate offices. In 1907, 724 offences were recorded. Prosecutions were only taken after repeated warnings, In other cases, offenders were merely given a printed copy of the by-laws. It is interesting that this system of education, visits, advice and warnings followed eventually by prosecution, where wilful and prolonged illegality occurs, has endured.

The Employment of Children Act 1903 also allowed local authorities to make by-laws, which Bradford duly did. Children under the age of 11 were no longer allowed to work as street traders and children employed in public entertainment needed a licence. During 1906, 61 children were licensed to perform. Visits to check on theatres found a number of unlicensed children employed in "bloodless surgery demonstrations" and "electrical performances", which sounds as though their limbs, if not their lives, would be at risk.

Another child's act was considered so dangerous that the chief of police was contacted in the next town where the troupe was due to perform. One poor creature was employed as a ballet girl in the pantomime as well as being a part-timer in a factory. When she was on the early shift at the factory, her hours were from 6 am until 11 pm. Her father had lied to the theatre about her age (he said she was over 14) so he was prosecuted with a fine of 20s or 10 days in jail. He chose the latter.

Canal boats were another area of concern with captains needing encouragement to look after their crews on the Leeds to Liverpool. Inspectors checked conditions of ventilation, lack of water, insanitary water tanks and overcrowding. A major problem was water leaking through bulkheads onto bunks where the crew slept. Normally, a caution was all that was required to get improvements made, but if this did not work notices were served. In 1903, 26 canal boats needed improving and one captain, who wouldn't let the inspector on his boat, was prosecuted for obstruction: the fine was £1.

The battle for clean air continued up to and past the Edwardian period. The mill chimneys could turn day into night. The 1901 health report stated: "It is a matter of regret that, in spite of diligent attention on the part of the Smoke Inspector, the condition of the atmosphere in Bradford has not of late undergone any appreciable difference."

During a coal strike in 1902, the people of Bradford saw their city in a new light as the mill chimneys shut down – Bradfordians could see the other side of the valley for the first time.

Ice cream makers (676 visits in 1903) and fried fish shops (666 visits) were particular worries from both food safety and nuisance points of view. In the summer, visits were made to the Italian quarters to check on ice cream makers in situ. The health committee's attention had been drawn to the "disgusting and dirty conditions" prevailing in fish shops on several occasions and, in one case, observed "filthy shops, dirty pans, foul smelling cellars and a WC compartment opening directly onto the room where the fish and potatoes were stored". By 1911, progress had been made in fish shops, which appeared in Britain in the 1850s, as open pans were replaced by new sanitary ranges.

The results of 1904's food and drug sampling programme noted that amongst the usual adulterations of milk, beer and butter, a sample of Paregoric did not contain enough opium, but as the label stated "without opium", the council could not prosecute. In 1905, though, a sample of laudanum failed, due to it only having two-thirds the correct amount of morphine, so there was serious trouble for the errant chemist.

In 1906, alarms were created by allegations concerning American tinned food and a good number of these products were tested. They were all free from impurities, except a sample of bottled peas that had some copper in it, but this fault had also been declared on the label, so it was okay.

The 1904 annual report contained the rules applying to the tenancies of new workmen's dwellings that had been built in Faxfleet Street. No pigeons or poultry were permitted and "no cotton waste, cotton or anything else likely to choke the drain" was allowed to be put down the toilet. Security of tenure was minimal. If told to leave on rent day – because you had, for example, been putting pigeons down the toilet – you had to be out by the next rent day. By 1911, two new inspectors had been appointed to look at the housing of the working classes and they had done some sterling work, with just over 1,000 inspections each in the year and more than 1,000 nuisances discovered.

The annual report of 1905 notes that money has been raised for a council crematorium. The crematorium movement, which considered burning as the most satisfactory way of disposing of the dead (see appendix one), would regularly write to local authorities encouraging them to build crematoria and to encourage their populations to use them. The first municipal crematorium was in Woking in 1885.

Bradford's was not particularly popular. Only 12 people were cremated in 1905, 13 in 1906 and 14 the year after. This was out of 4,202 deaths. If the relatives didn't want them, the ashes were deposited in a niche in something called the "columbarium". The annual report of the Cremation Society of Great Britain claimed in 1907 that its favoured method was "undoubtedly the best method of disposing of the bodies of the dead". But most people did not agree. You can almost hear a sigh as the report observes: "The progress of any reform which touches a traditional sentiment must always be slow." Yorkshire could be proud, however, that in the number of crematoria it stood "easily first among the counties of Great Britain".

B radford always had major problems with infant mortality. The death rate for babies was usually the second highest in the country and in the Edwardian period thought to be caused by a number of factors including ill-fed mothers, inappropriate infant feeding and the ill-regulated profession of midwifery. In 1901, an important decision had been made: "The sub-committee in view of the information obtained from other large towns on this subject, are fully assured of the good results to be obtained by an appointment of this nature." What was this radical new appointment? What would make the influential health committee of the City of Bradford seek assurances from other authorities, rather than just getting on with things as it had done before, with radical measures like the introduction of public housing and school meals? It was the employment of a female. The committee took the risk and a Miss Stevens, who held a certificate from the Sanitary Institute, was duly appointed as a sanitary inspector.

In the annual report, her name was added at the bottom of the list of the department's employees. She followed the clerks and store-keeper in the natural order of importance. She and her subsequent colleagues (as she proved to be worthy of the risk the committee took) retained this position at the bottom of the list throughout the decade. Two other members of staff were added that year. They were male clerks whose duties, amongst other things, were to "make themselves generally useful about the department": a phrase dropped from job descriptions nowadays, perhaps unwisely.

By 1902, because of the hard work of Miss Stevens, another woman was taken on. Their work was mainly on overcrowded dwellings and the inspection of workplaces where women were employed. The women sanitary inspectors (always misses – perhaps it was too soon to appoint a married woman) were particularly important in the regulation of midwives. There was a Midwives Act of 1902 and the sanitary inspectors not only registered midwives but action was taken in cases of ignorance or dereliction of duty.

By March 1905, all women wanting to practise as midwives had to be enrolled with the Central Midwives Board. Unfortunately, only 30 of the 101 women in Bradford known to be midwives had done so. Of those, only four were fully trained, the remainder being "more or less ignorant, some being unable to sign their name, and all have little or no knowledge of the use of disinfectants". Seventy needed twice-weekly visits to check on them, allowing instruction on cleanliness and the use of basic equipment. A special section in the 1905 report allowed the full spleen of the medical officer of health to be vented. He observed that "only six might be described as satisfactory", "most are very ignorant" and "very few recognise the importance of cleanliness, having no practical knowledge of disinfection".

Most damning of all perhaps was a single paragraph that merely stated "eight are women of doubtful moral character". A later tome, Aids to Public Health, helpfully assisted in the assessment of people's mental and moral states. It gave sanitary officers a useful guide on four grades of mental deficiency. Officers could decide whether people were idiots, imbeciles, feeble-minded or, even worse, moral defectives.

There was a discussion in the 1905 report on the deaths of babies from diarrhoeal disease. Only a few died in the first month. This was because after that, the infant's natural food, mother's milk, received "considerable additions in the shape of bread crumbs, artificial foods, and occasionally tea and bread and butter". Wasting diseases, however, did kill a lot of the very young – they were thought to have been born in such a malnourished, weakly condition that they were unable to cope with "extra-uterine existence".

A 1906 conference held in Bradford called for radical measures. Maternity leave should be extended from one month to three. School-girls should be trained in motherhood duties and the Midwives Act should be extended to include Scotland and Ireland. The confer-ence also suggested baby minders should be regulated, as they often had "improper conditions". It decided that the Dairies, Cowsheds and Milk Shops Order was defective and its provisions should be extended to cover dirty milk and allow the authorities to prosecute where milk was impure.

There were a surprising number of these establishments. In 1905, Bradford had 387 registered cow keepers, 650 cowsheds, 519 milk vendors and 169 people selling milk in the street. Almost a thousand visits to cowsheds were made the autumn of 1906, with the results that the town clerk wrote to all cowshed owners reminding them of the regulations requiring lime washing and cleansing at least twice a year. This was not happening. The committee had instructed him to write to tell them that: "No warnings will be given, as in the past" but that "Proceeding will be instituted whenever a breach… is detected."

The annual report's introductory comments for 1905 are inter-esting. Infant deaths were still high: "Economic conditions largely account for these (upward) changes. When the men are out of work, women are forced to earn the livelihood, the infants being then entirely weaned… In many cases malnutrition is responsible for the mothers having insufficient milk." Three deaths were due to prematurity that year; no other comment was made other than "two of these being illegitimate children". The final comments deserve to be repeated in full: "A very large proportion of the mothers, whose infants died, were of the careless, neglectful type, and six were obliged to go out to work, leaving the infant in charge of an ignorant woman." Presumably they got all they deserved, then.

A newly-created post of midwife inspector saw a Miss Hall start in September 1906. The report of her first term noted that, as well as "disinfectants being largely absent during births", "the great number of midwives seemed to think they had done all that was necessary if they washed their hands after attending a confinement". They all (with the exception of "six who were over 70 years old") had a bag with the necessary scissors, nailbrush, soap and thermometer, even though not many actually used them. Miss Hall's boss noted that, "The superstitious and erroneous ideas which exist as to the causes and cures of the various affections to which the lying-in woman and her newly born child are liable are so deeply rooted that rational midwifery will not take place for some time to come."

There was a Notification of Births Act in 1907, which improved the situation, as official notifications allowed for earlier visits to the mother and child. By 1911, the inspectors considered that more than 90 per cent of births were being notified. This not only picked up problems more quickly but also allowed sanitary inspectors to give information to mothers about hygiene and breast-feeding. Advice included going to the humanised milk depot, if the mother found she was unable to feed her new infant.

Set up by the council in 1903, the facility provided humanised milk in sterilised bottles with clean teats. A Cinderella Club of volunteers helped with the distribution. Unfortunately, the 1906 report noted: "It is a matter of regret (that) sometimes the milk is decanted from the bottle into a foul smelling feeding bottle." Although it was not the best milk (only mothers' milk was that), it was far superior to "the sour material administered by a dirty bottle and a long India rubber feeding tube". By 1911, nearly 186,000 bottles of humanised milk were being sold. Interestingly, the year before, the number had been 242,000 and the year after 312,000; why the amount dropped in that warm year is not made clear.

Times were changing, but only slowly. In 1911, more than half of the 20,000 nationally registered midwives were untrained. Sometimes, unregistered midwives attended births. But even if this was discovered, the department had difficulties proving that it had not just been done in an emergency. The act of 1902 required them to prove that the midwife was acting "habitually and for gain". Another situation that led to prosecutions was when a midwife carried out an abortion, rather than a birth.

A welfare issue that often exercised the minds of the health department was half-day closing. In those days, shopkeepers in specific trades asked the council for a vote among their fellow tradesmen on whether to introduce a standard half-day or not. This not only gave them a rest on half a day, but also made sure they all closed at the same time, so no one stole anyone else's customers.

In 1907, hairdressers and butchers asked for this to happen. Votes were taken and the overwhelming majority (it had to be at least two-thirds according to the Shop Hours Act 1904) voted for, and got, a half-day (Tuesday). Of course, as soon as it was made, people wanted to be exempted. Many shops in the central area wanted to stay open all the time and 29 pork butchers complained about being included in any order along with "ordinary butchers".

Closing hours for butchers – pork or otherwise – became 7 pm on Monday and Wednesday, 1 pm on Tuesday, 8 pm on Thursday, 10 pm on Friday and midnight on Saturday. Living next to a butcher's shop must have been a tad annoying if customers were queuing up until midnight on Saturdays. Night visits during 1907 found 49 shops operating outside these hours. Four, after repeated warnings, were prosecuted. The year after, there was a call for a general closing order for all shops. The vote was indecisive, so it didn't happen.

In the appendices of the report for 1911 were two sections, one for each of the sexes working for the department. There were eight women sanitary inspectors by this time (working mainly on reducing infant mortality) but still only two male inspectors working under the Shops Hours Acts, the Employment of Children Act, the Prevention of Cruelty to Children Act and the sanitary provisions of the Factory and Workshop Act.

The head male was Frank White – superintendent and chief inspector of nuisances. One of his major worries was the offensive trades that caused untold misery to their neighbourhoods. As well as the delightful-sounding grease extractors, fell mongers, gut scrapers, artificial manure makers and rabbit skin dryers were India rubber makers, gas makers and fish fryers.

The canal boat inspector was now required to inspect common lodging houses as well. There were 35 in Bradford, with a total of 137 sleeping rooms containing 1,793 beds, with a nightly average of 1,421 inmates during the year. This meant that there were more than 100 occupants per room. In 1911, inspectors made 2,000 day-visits but only four night inspections. A reluctance to turn out after dark may be understandable – the places they visited were dangerous and five of them needed fumigating during the year. The lodging houses were indescribably overcrowded, serving a travelling population of vagrants moving from town to town, looking for work. A report from the previous century talked of what happened when all the beds were full. If there were customers left, ropes were strung across the room at chest height. For a small fee, you could cross your arms over the rope and try to get some sleep.

What else was happening at the end of the Edwardian period, in this seething and sulphurous city? The annual report noted that there had been a high presence of zymotic diarrhoea, due to an "unusually hot dry summer". In a time of insanitary food preparation, little or no refrigeration and dubious water supplies, it is little wonder that food-related illnesses proliferated in hot summers. There were also increase in infant mortality and typhoid fever, just as Typhoid Mary was sensationally being let out of her solitary confinement on the other side of the Atlantic, ready to resume the only trade she knew – cooking.

There was obviously a long way to go, with many areas of health, safety and welfare absent from the statute books. If you were not in a specific profession or trade and you weren't a young person or a lady shop-worker, the scant legislation may not have applied to you. What little progress there was had been hard fought for by sanitary inspectors. Huge number of visits, discussions, exhortations and, in some cases, prosecutions had been made by stalwart officers, both male and female, in the overcrowded and dangerous world of Bradford in Edwardian times.

*David Clapham*

# CHAPTER 4

# The Women Inspectors

*It is not everyone who can deal satisfactorily with others. The woman who is most likely to be able to do so is one who belongs to a class which has always been accustomed to exercising a certain amount of authority over others, therefore, the official position will not come to her as an entirely new thing and she will not be so liable to consider herself of too much importance and, on that account, to patronise those who she visits. Not only will she have dealing with the working classes, with tradesmen and with manufacturers, but also with voluntary workers of often high social standing.*

*Edith L. Maynard,*
*Women in the Public Health Service, 1915*

The women sanitary inspectors of a century ago were courageous, committed, hardworking and most were extremely well-qualified. Successful women examinees commonly outnumbered men and often did better than them. In 1911, 40,000 demonstrated in London in support of women's suffrage, working people across the UK engaged in major strikes and protests seeking better conditions, and the first National Insurance Act was passed, creating the foundation of the modern welfare state as we know it. The very air was abuzz with good, progressive possibilities. But fewer than 15 years later, the profession was almost exclusively male once more. At a time when there were signs of such promising changes in so many fields, whatever happened to cause these superior "lady inspectors" to go into the profession and then to be lost from it?

Edwardian England was a complex setting for social developments, building as it did on the moralising and hypocrisy of the Victorian era. The extension of the work of sanitary inspectors to women came about partly because of Victorian attitudes that only women could talk to women about sanitation. It was also made possible because within Edwardian society, there was so much aspiration, so much energy and idealism, and because improved education for girls had resulted in pools of talented young women who longed to go out into the world and work.

Middle-class women might still be brought up with an expectation that their main role would be as mothers, nurturing, teaching and nursing their own children, but some were benefiting from an improved educational system and a few girls' schools were even sending pupils to universities and colleges. Some of these women did take up careers, although if they married, they would generally have to return to the non-working state, dependent on their husbands for their homes and hearths (in 1911, only one in 10 wives from all classes was employed). The range of professions was limited, however; there was indignation at the idea of middle-class women taking up occupations seen as unnatural for their sex, even if, as unmarried women, or "spinsters", they desperately needed the money. The culture and understandings of refined women were seen as quite separate and specialised to those of men; their place was not in the workplace or the polling station, but in a moral, companionable sphere, away from the vulgar, grasping or unpleasant.

Yet, alongside the ingrained ideas of what was proper for the weaker, cleaner sex to do, the Edwardian spirit was aspirational and exploratory, and determined to use science and modern approaches to bring about a better world. Many kinds of changes were stirring: social, political and economic. Sections of the intelligentsia had long been part of what was called the "public health movement", hoping to improve the terrible conditions in the slums and factories. Many of them were involved in philanthropic work of various kinds, and writers such as Charles Kingsley were active in trying to effect change.

The National Health Society, for example, had been founded in the 1870s to promote health amongst all classes, especially by education. It encouraged women to train as teachers, presenting prizes and medals to the successful (it was well-funded, for it had three princesses as patrons) and in 1899 it began a course for lady sanitary inspectors that would equip them to take the same examinations as men. A similar spirit led to a trickle of articles in the women's magazines of the day, advising and encouraging young women as to how they might take up paid occupations.

For example, consider this small selection: Fraser's Magazine carried an article in 1877 on women dentists, the Women's Gazette in 1888 on managing an elementary school, the Young Woman, 1899, on being a legal typist and the Imperial Colonist, 1908, on horticulture as a career for women. In 1898, Isabella Ormston Ford wrote "Women as Factory Inspectors and Certifying Surgeons", and four years later, the National Council of Women of Great Britain published "Women as Sanitary Inspectors". One can imagine young women sitting at home and dreaming of a meaningful, independent life, perhaps assisting in remedying some of the social wrongs they saw around them, and wondering how they might begin and what their parents might say.

Public health: women were often employed in roles involving children

Slowly, from the 1870s onwards, women had begun to be employed in tasks that the state, national or local, needed to have done. Naturally, given Victorian attitudes as to what was their forte, the work generally involved oversight of conditions for working-class women or children. At a national level, a handful of women took appointments inspecting pauper schools, tenements or fostering services. Remarkably, there is a record that in Glasgow, in 1877, six women were appointed as assistant sanitary inspectors to inspect tenement housing.

By the 1890s, in Britain, hundreds of thousands of working women were doing hard and unrelenting work for long hours in factories, workshops and sweatshops, often in very bad conditions. At the time there was, as later, a complicated setting out of jurisdiction between national and local inspectorates, and no clear distinction between factories and workshops. Commonly, the relatively few inspections carried out would have been done by male sanitary inspectors, and they were far too few for the task. The Royal Commission on Labour in 1892 included four lady assistant commissioners (two of them trade unionists), who investigated working conditions for women, getting some help from local philanthropic ladies' societies.

The women visited hundreds of workplaces and witnessed a vast range of problems. There were workplaces infested with rats, dangerously long hours worked and high levels of dust, heat and steam, but particularly relevant was the shocking state of the lavatories and washing facilities. One inspector described the "filth and offensive odours" of lavatories cleaned "twice a year". Some sanitary accommodation for women was directly off workrooms, often without doors or bolts. Testimony from a member of the Ropeworkers' Union vividly described how most women workers never saw a sanitary inspector and could not talk freely to a man about sanitary conditions.

The commission's final report led to the passing of the groundbreaking Factories and Workshops Act in 1892, which extended protection for workers in many ways. It created many duties for local authorities regarding, for example, overcrowding, ventilation and heating, and transferred responsibility for sanitary conditions in factories and workshops to them. It became an offence, for example, to employ persons "in places injurious to health". There were particular requirements as to sanitary conditions where women worked. Victorian attitudes towards women were quite separate from Victorian attitudes towards making money, and whilst it was considered perfectly reasonable for women "of the lower class" to work each day until they were exhausted, poor sanitary provision was considered a threat to their health and morals, and it was accepted that this was, between men and women, a highly embarrassing and improper topic. Asquith, then the responsible minister, after much lobbying by women, took the almost unprecedented step of appointing women as factory inspectors, because "there could not be free and frank communications between female operatives on the one side and the male inspector on the other" and, afraid to be specific, pointed to "the intuitive and instinctive knowledge" which women inspectors would have about the problems of other women.

Within a year, the Borough of Kensington had appointed two women as workshop inspectors – Miss Lucy Deane and Miss Rose Squire – and Misses May Abraham and Mary Paterson were made the first lady factory inspectors. A separate branch of the Factory Inspectorate was created especially for them, as their presence was considered so extraordinary and potentially threatening. They were soon joined by Miss Adelaide Mary Anderson in Leeds. In Nottingham, too, Miss Hawksley was appointed woman inspector of workshops. Whilst we have names and a few details of these early women pioneers, we know comparatively little about them: they were reticent, their job titles varied and few local authorities have kept records about them. Whilst there are some lively accounts of the doings of the first women factory inspectors, most of our knowledge of the women sanitary inspectors' lives comes from talks they gave (inevitably rather formal) and the continuing correspondence about them in the Sanitary Journal. Edith Maynard, whose words head this chapter, was unusual in writing two books, one on health and safety in china works and one on the situation of women inspectors, but she gave few personal details of what their lives were like.

The next few years brought a sprinkling of women's appointments over a much wider area, but encouragement for their work seemed to be matched with evidence of resentment: by 1896, Kensington, Islington, St. Pancras and Southwark vestries (the unit of local government then) in London had appointed women sanitary inspectors. In 1897, however, two (unnamed) women inspectors tried to become members of the Sanitary Inspectors' Association and this caused outrage. A year later, Miss Alice Billings was appointed "Sanitary Inspectress" for West Ham. By 1900, Leeds, Bradford, Sheffield and St Helens had all appointed women as assistant inspectors of nuisances. In 1901, Miss Margaret Sharples from Leeds was even admitted into the men's Sanitary Inspectors' Association, then based in Victoria Street in London. Often, it was forward-thinking and influential local medical officers of health who were behind the women's appointments. The work the women did and the payment they received varied across the country. Some – Leeds was a shining example – did equivalent work to the men and received the same salary. In many areas, however, the role perceived as appropriate for them by the men was heavily qualified. Correspondence published in The Sanitary Journal for the years 1904 to 1910 shows clearly that there was strong resistance to women doing work in abattoirs, for example. Doubts about what it was wise to ask them to do reinforced councillors' concerns at costs; most women were paid significantly less than men. Local authorities that could would appoint them as health visitors, at salaries of less than £100 a year. The highest paid probably received around £150; £180 was possible with London weighting.

Many of these women would now be called high-flyers. They generally held equivalent (or higher) qualifications to their male counterparts. The women appointed in Leeds, for example, all held sanitary certificates; the first was also trained in obstetrics, the second had a BA degree and the third had a nursing qualification. Most doing home visits would have additional nursing or midwifery quali-fications and some had degrees. Several left for illustrious careers elsewhere, as is explored later.

Ominously for the future of women sanitary inspectors, theirs was not the only work role for women in the field of public health. Phil-anthropic and Christian work over several decades had established a system of health visiting whereby middle-class women (earlier, most had been working class), using tact and feminine understanding, would explain to poor mothers "in the way of a wise friend" topics such as how to use carbolic powder and the importance of fresh air, cleanliness, thrift, temperance and nursing the sick.

Their role, which overlapped with part of the work of the women sanitary inspectors, had become much more valued after the shocking discovery at the time of the Boer War that many working men were too puny to enlist and it came to be appreciated how vital it was that children should be brought up strong and healthy. As the role was developed, so more women trained for it. The Journal of the Royal Sanitary Institute reported in 1904 that: "There are plenty of excel-lently qualified women eagerly seeking for posts as health visitors."

Originally, much health visiting had been voluntary, but gradually, across many local authorities, paid work became available and so some middle-class women, working under medical officers of health, had slipped, as it were, into the modern position of being paid for advising the lower orders.

In terms of Edwardian society, it was a marriage made in heaven, for the widespread perception was that working-class women were ignorant (and feckless) and in need of guidance, and health visitors were perfectly schooled in such a role. They fitted well into departments where middle-class, respectable men were employed, complementing and not challenging their work, and the women sanitary inspectors seem to have treated them as valuable colleagues, although their qualifications were much lower than their own. There was also a key difference in approach, as anyone who has worked in environmental health today will testify.

An inspector's work is done very much with the attitude of an investigator, who brings reason, science, and knowledge of existing law and social mores to bear on problems to try to improve matters, using the legal system when necessary. The approach of a health visitor was essentially that of a sympathetic and understanding visitor to the house, who would try to impart knowledge to the individual mother in a personal way. While the women sanitary inspectors used a good deal of tact, their upstart"serving of legal notices in particular was galling to many of their male colleagues.

Writing in the Sanitary Journal in 1910, a male inspector, Francis Vacher, accepted, somewhat grudgingly, that women sanitary inspectors could be deployed in some circumstances but only "in comparatively extensive districts... where the local industry necessitates the employment of a large proportion of women and girls". He considered that they could usefully inspect workshops where women and children were employed and common lodging houses taking women, take records of infant deaths, and inspect houses let in lodgings, remarking: "In our town I know the female inspector visits houses let in lodgings soon after breakfast and sees that the children are well washed, and the beds made, and the rooms ventilated." He reiterated that: "The woman is not, now, and never will be, the rival of the man." What a joy it must have been to work with him.

The male inspectors' lack of welcome to the women was only partly based on prejudice: there was already an oversupply of sanitary inspectors (of whatever sex) and having invested in training, and with their own wives and families to support, many of the men must have felt worried and determined to remove the threat of being displaced. An anonymous male sanitary inspector protested to the Sanitary Record claiming that women inspectors made "absurd and unnecessary enquiries", and exaggerated small problems while ignoring big ones. Tellingly, he refers to them as "Lady Health Visitors" and argues that they should work in a separate sphere from the male sanitary inspector. His remarks are reminiscent of judgements directed by a male sports commentator on the first woman linesman working in the premier league in January, 2011. How attitudes endure!

Being a pioneer might have its rewards but it must have been cheerless to return home from a town hall, where women would know they were resented, and to live, generally alone, probably in a couple of rooms, on a very low salary. The work was sometimes searingly hard. To quote Edith Maynard, chief woman sanitary inspector of Leeds: "Because there were so few women inspectors only the most wretched neighbourhoods were covered, and there, they had to persuade people in poverty to abandon long-established, embedded practices." Writing in 1915, she warned that a new woman inspector needed initiative and to "have many resources in herself and to be a great reader, if she is not to become depressed from the inevitable isolation of the life".

The women sanitary inspectors, when empowered by their local authorities (for their contracts varied), inspected a wide range of premises, including dairies and markets, and most especially workshops where women worked. They would check notification of infectious diseases, tracing and then visiting the sick persons' workplaces or schools, to try to prevent spread of infection. After the passing of the Factory Act of 1901, their work also covered outworkers based at home. Yet the bulk of their time was taken up with what was disparagingly termed "baby work".

One of their chief tasks was to visit midwives when at their work and try to improve their standards. The extremely poor level of practice can be gauged by statistics of the time. A contemporary Italian-born economist and MP, L.G. Chiozza-Money, estimated that between a quarter and a third of the babies born in 1911 were "born to want and squalor" in conditions of extreme poverty, and that, on average across the country, 120 babies in 1,000 died under the age of one; in some of the poorer wards of some cities, such as Birmingham, one in three babies was dying.

Many of the midwives could not write and most knew very little about disinfectants. For those pregnant women who could not afford midwives, there were untrained "handy women". These were forbidden by law to practise without a doctor other than in an emergency. This illegal status meant that they were difficult to track down and few would admit to working. To quote one inspector, "to question a patient about her nurse was like treading on thin ice, yet it often had to be done." With no right of entry under the legislation on midwifery, the woman sanitary inspector had to impress by sheer personality. Advice on regular feeding and suitable foods might be met with a scornful: "Well, I've buried eight so I ought to know."

A good deal of our knowledge about this aspect of their work comes from Bradford (see chapter three) – in particular, the reports of the full-time midwifery specialist there, Miss Jones. One of her records gives an instant appreciation of the gross quality of some of the situations: "We entered a house in the centre of the city, where, after some conversation with the midwife, we requested her to produce her syringe; this was duly brought, wrapped up in brown paper, which on being opened was found to be infested with bugs, which the woman in her confusion brushed towards us."

Miss Jones' experience led her to believe that a third of the infant deaths in Bradford in 1908 were caused by "prematurity, atrophy or debility" and that the high rates of prematurity may have been from "wilful attempts to procure abortion" because of "fear of poverty". Her reports gave vivid details of desperately poor women giving birth, assisted only by kind neighbours, and their pathetic efforts to deal with the new infant when they had to resume working. Miss Jones called for a municipal maternity home and a home help service, yet many Bradford councillors were unsympathetic and thought that "the union" (the poorhouse service) was quite sufficient public provision as a fall-back for the very poor. Women inspectors also had to attend inquests into babies' deaths, which must have been heart-breaking.

A related role was giving advice on the feeding and care of infants and children, and here the work overlapped with that of health visitors. This could be hard work: "It required great strength of character and perseverance to attempts to reform [the feeding of] even an infant of six weeks old when the attempt resulted in much crying." And, at a time when eugenics was highly respected, the women inspectors' accounts of their work emphasised they were not trying "to keep alive diseased babies who might be better dead, although that might sometimes be the result – but rather to see to it that more children grew up to be healthy, straight-limbed individuals." With such enormous tasks and often as the sole woman inspector in a local authority, it was only to be expected that the women would organise and try to improve their situation.

In London, a small group of women working on public health started meeting together in 1896. Gradually, the meetings grew bigger. By 1902, minutes were being taken and by 1904 rules were agreed. In 1906, the membership was set as women sanitary inspectors or health visitors (who were in the minority), and opened out to those in the provinces, Sixty-three women were recorded as members and later, there would be around 200. The aims of the new Women's Sanitary Inspectors' Association (WSIA) were to: "Safeguard the interests and improve the status of women public health workers and to promote the interchange of relevant technical and professional knowledge." We know that one of their activities was monitoring legislation and liaising with women across the labour movement on all areas of public health work, from working conditions and nuisance to infant nutrition.

However lofty the association, in many local authorities, it was likely that women sanitary inspectors would be being paid less than men, or as health visitors, at even lower rates. In 1910, the WSIA successfully fended off a bill that would have enabled new health visitors to be employed on low salaries and with no stipulated qualifications.

Yet the problems endured – local authorities continued to appoint health visitors and to pay them at low rates. By 1913, Florence Greenwood recorded an "almost complete cessation" of the appointment of women sanitary inspectors. Further legislation on maternity and child welfare in 1914 and 1915, which gave powers to levy a rate to cover infant welfare, increasingly tipped the balance towards health visitors being appointed, and the advisory role for women being preferred. The First World War made things even harder. The WSIA merged with the Health Visitors Association in 1915. Thus, within a generation, the male sanitary inspectors' domain was as if it had never been threatened by female counterparts.

Women sanitary inspectors were modest and, apart from the formal records of their organisation, very little is known about them personally or their careers. It was a different matter for some of the women who left the profession, some of whom had amazing adventures. In particular, Charlotte Marsh became a prominent suffragette and Rose Squire, after adventures in the Factory Inspectorate, a high-level civil servant.

Suffragettes – generally extremists and far from the main stream – were at the height of their influence in 1910 and 1911. Charlotte Marsh was the member of the movement with the closest connection to the profession of public health. She was described by a contemporary as a "strikingly beautiful girl with blue eyes and long, corn-coloured hair". Affected by the appalling conditions in which she had seen women living and working, she became one of the first women ever to train to become a sanitary inspector, but then left to become a full time organiser of the Women's Social and Political Union (WSPU) in March 1908.

Marsh was arrested for obstructing the police in Parliament Square the same year and sentenced to a month in Holloway. She was one of the first women to be force-fed and to endure the "cat and mouse" game of releasing women when they became too weak and re-arresting them when their strength returned. Because of her beautiful hair, she was chosen to be a standard bearer at many suffragette marches and processions, including serving as cross-bearer for the funeral of Emily Davidson, who had been her close friend (Davidson, famously, was fatally injured beneath the hooves of King George V's horse at the Epsom Derby of 1913). Later, she trained as a motor mechanic and sometimes acted as chauffeur to Mrs Pankhurst.

At the outbreak of war in 1914, the suffragettes agreed to end all militant actions and to support the war effort. Agreeing with this policy at first, Charlotte Marsh became chauffeur to David Lloyd George, who suggested to her that it would "promote the victory of the cause of women's enfranchisement". Later, (presumably disillusioned), she worked as a member of the Women's Land Army. During the war, she and others became critical of the direction of the movement. In 1916, she was a founder of a new independent WSPU. After the war, she worked for the Women's International League for Peace and Freedom in the United States and, later, in the Public Assistance department of the London County Council during the so-called "lean thirties", often making friends with her clients.

After her death, Dorothy Bowker wrote of how they first met, "when we were both in Aylesbury Gaol for window-smashing. Her gaiety and invincible spirit inspired me, as I am sure it did the other 38 prisoners there. In the dark hours of hunger and thirst strikes and forcible feeding, her courage shone through it all and helped me to fight to the last gasp."

Another pioneer, Rose Squire, the daughter of a Harley Street doctor, was one of the first women sanitary inspectors to be appointed. She had been educated by governesses and had made her debut at court. Unexpectedly finding herself in need of an income, she went to work. From the first, her accuracy and keenness were remarkable. Her observations on conditions in laundries, as observed by a sanitary inspector, were used in the amendments to the Factory Act in 1896.

In 1895, she was invited to join the Factory Inspectorate and took the civil service examination as the only candidate. She recalled writing the exam in a room full of empty desks, watched by two men. She passed, joining as a lady inspector in 1896.

She travelled alone throughout Britain as part of her work, often incognito, much to the disapproval of her relatives and friends. Sir Malcolm Delevingne recalled the travels of the peripatetic lady inspectors as being "as thrilling as any to be found in the pages of Malory". The women, he tells us, set out on trains and bicycles, in Irish jaunting cars, and on foot to do battle against "health hazards, industrial dangers, [and] excessive hours".

Squire loved being involved in prosecutions. On one occasion, she investigated a "well-known Regent Street shop" in which the staff were required to stay on after shop hours to fill orders and pack chocolates in fine boxes with delicate papers and ribbons. During the Christmas season, this meant them working very late. Squire raided the shop after midnight to gain evidence, the shop girls being delighted at her entrance.

In court, the defence argued that packing an elaborate box was no different from putting groceries into a sack. Rose Squire had bought, and brought to court, one of the boxes of the chocolates, "beautiful with its gorgeous and skilfully tied bow". She notes: "This brilliant object in the drab police court, and later at the Court of King's Bench, caused no little amusement and much enlivened the proceedings." The Chief Justice ruled in Squire's favour and the lady inspectors shared the contents of the box in celebration.

Later, she travelled to Ireland. She went undercover, staying in a fishing hotel on the coast of County Donegal and tried, unsuccessfully as it turned out, to bring a successful prosecution against a "gombeen man" who paid women a pittance (in the currency of stock from his own shop) for knitting socks. Squire collected information about this illegal local economy but John Sweeney, the shopkeeper, was also a county councillor and very influential, and the case, although brought twice, was dismissed.

In 1918, Squire moved to the Ministry of Munitions as director of women's welfare. By that year, more than 240,000 women were placed away from home to work on munitions. Her officers visited the factories, "largely managed by autocratic military officers", to enforce welfare standards. There were concerns about the women's housing and food and, in the factories, the perpetual risks of explosion and industrial poisoning: the explosive TNT caused the women's skin to turn yellow, some dying from the poisoning, others suffering toxic symptoms, such as anorexia, swelling of hands and feet, and long-term drowsiness. In the last stage of her career, she moved to the Industrial Division of the Home Office, working on policy planning, retiring in 1926.

They may have not been treated fairly, yet one must be glad what these and many other women attempted so many years ago, and we can be proud of what they achieved. As Maynard put it in 1915: "In no profession can the worker feel more strongly that she is really affecting something... she does not inspect workshops, outworkers, offices, etc. merely in order to perfunctorily enforce certain requirements of the law, but to improve the physical and moral conditions of the workers; she does not inspect midwives merely to see that the bare letter of the law... is complied with, but to help the mother and the child – to save life, protect health and increase comfort; she does not visit infants and the home generally merely to fill in certain forms and to report or deal with nuisances, but to actually stem the tide of infant mortality, limit the number of cripples... help the harassed mother and increase the comfort in the home for the hardworking father." Bravo!

*Ava Greenwell*

# CHAPTER 5

# The Home

*House No. 4. Two rooms. Seven inmates. Walls, ceiling and furniture filthy. Dirty flock bedding in living room placed on a box and two chairs. Smell in room from dirt and bad air unbearable, and windows and door closed. There is no through ventilation in this house. Children pale, starved-looking, and only half-clothed. One boy with hip disease, another with sores over face.*

*B. Seebohm Rowntree, Poverty: A Study of Town Life, 1902*

Housing policy may well represent the pinnacle of Edwardian social and political change, reaching its finale with the Lloyd George-inspired "homes fit for heroes" building push in the aftermath of the First World War and – for the first time – state-funded council housing. The late Victorian and Edwardian era's housing developments were many, as links between housing and health were increasingly recognised, largely due to the poor health of soldiers in the Boer War (and later First World War) and the perceived need for a healthy industrial workforce. The main housing providers were private builders, who required a return on their investment (which was not always forthcoming); factory owners, who required a productive, healthy and compliant workforce; and philanthropists, who saw that the poor needed someone to help them, provision being subject to the philanthropist's own values and morals.

Let's start with how housing standards were changing for the new middles classes in the Edwardian era (or those of the "new money", quite a distinct class from the landed gentry). These emerging middle-class households were beginning to benefit from a burgeoning consumer age and the home improvements of the day. One might, by now, expect a scullery off a small kitchen – a hygienic separation of workspaces for cooking, and the cleaning of clothes and dishes – and, possibly, an inside bathroom.

The kitchen may have had a coal-fired range for cooking and heating (much heat was provided by coal fires), or a gas oven, probably hired, which would have been easier to clean and more reliable. To keep food cool, larders had mesh windows, although iceboxes had become available in the late Victorian period.

Many of the middle classes still had a washstand in their bedrooms and bathed in a tin bath in front of a fire, although plumbed baths were becoming available. One was offered by Harrods in 1901 for £5, comprising a geyser attached to a tinned steel bath.

Outside WCs remained popular, to help separate all those embarrassing, unspoken tasks completed with torn sheets of newspaper. The poorest often shared an outside privy, equipped with a flushing toilet or earth or pail closet.

Inside and outside the home, gas lighting was gradually being replaced by the new-fangled electricity, although it was expensive until after the First World War and generally only available to better-off families. Most households retained gas lighting, supplemented by oil lamps and candles.

With electricity in the home would come still-rudimentary appliances – the electric iron, fires, kettles, washing machines, hairdryers and, even, vacuum-cleaners. Such items were a real boost, as domestic servants – particularly women – were taking up opportunities for less gruelling and better-paid forms of work. At the turn of the century, there were 1.5 million women in domestic service to the upper and middle classes, leading an "upstairs downstairs" existence. They worked up to 17 hours per day, kept separate from the family by internal design. Some servants accompanied their employers to their other homes in the country or their seaside villas.

Novelist and biographer Margaret Forster documented her grandmother Margaret Ann's life as a domestic maid in Carlisle from around 1893: "Her annual wage, was eighteen pounds and her keep. She thought this keep good. She had her own room at the back of the house, above the scullery, overlooking the yard between the house and warehouse. It was small but it had a carpet on top of the linoleum, quite a luxury for a servant, a comfortable bed, a wardrobe and washstand, all fitted in somehow. There was a tiny wrought iron fireplace in which a few coals could be burned in the very cold weather (and there was plenty of that)."

Forster's mother, Lilian, (born in 1901) benefitted from social changes. She was bright, did well at school and secured a good job at the local public health department, until her marriage, when she gave up her work. Forster, in turn, benefitted from post-Second World War council housing and education in Carlisle, winning a scholarship to read history at Oxford. (We now know for certain that poor and overcrowded housing can severely affect a child's ability to reach their potential in education.)

Throughout the Victorian period, some 90 per cent of housing was privately rented and much of it was of very poor quality and insecure. Decent and affordable housing for the working classes, in both urban and rural locations, remained woefully inadequate and out of reach for most. Around a quarter of the urban population were struggling financially and a tenth could not even meet their basis needs. Half of farm labourers lived below the poverty line, often in one-roomed cottages with mud walls and no running water. Wages for the unskilled were low and irregular, and for private landlords, building and maintaining housing for the poor was not an attractive investment option.

So who was providing housing when the state was not? From the mid-19th century, some housing provision had come from factory owners, who recognised that better housed workers were more productive. One of the earliest was Titus Salt who, in 1850, built a complete village for his workers, consisting of a mill, housing, a hospital and school. The houses were laid out in small terraces in a grid pattern and had better sanitation and more space than earlier housing. The village was named after its founder and the river Aire, where the factory was located.

Because of its historical significance, it is now a much-visited Unesco world heritage site. A guidebook notes: "Saltaire, West Yorkshire, is a complete and well-preserved industrial village of the second half of the 19th century. Its textile mills, public buildings and workers' housing are built in a harmonious style of high architectural standards and the urban plan survives intact, giving a vivid impression of Victorian philanthropic paternalism."

Other "community towns" followed to encourage loyalty from employees through better housing. Port Sunlight, on the Wirral, was created by William Hesketh Lever for his Sunlight Soaps factory workers in 1888 and developed over the next 20 years with ornate house designs, gardens and wide roads, laid out on a deliberately irregular plan. Edwin Lutyens was one of the architects. It is now a museum and garden village.

Bournville village was developed from 1879 by two brothers, George and Richard Cadbury, Quakers and chocolate manufacturers, south of Birmingham. Its quality homes and gardens for "honest and sober workers" were close to the rail and canal networks. The settlement was built at the family's own expense to "alleviate the evils of modern more cramped living conditions". In 2003, it was said to be one of the "nicest places to live in Britain", although, more recently, in 2010, the community was concerned for its future following the takeover of Cadbury's by Kraft. Like Saltaire, Bournville is well documented and welcomes visitors.

At least poor housing conditions were being recognised and talked about, including by legislators. The Torrens and Cross Acts of the 1860s and 1870s were engines of slum improvement and clearance and contemporary medical officers of health undoubtedly saw improving housing as one of their fundamental roles. But they were aware that carrying out that role could lead to the poor being evicted and having to then choose between the streets or the workhouse.

The Public Health Act of 1875, which figures large in this book, contained important provisions giving householders powers over slum landlords. They were codified, in a useful document called The Tenant's Sanitary Catechism, produced by the Fabian Society in 1896. The catechism directs occupiers, if they feel their houses to be insanitary, to fill in the answers section and forward it to a sanitary inspector.

The document asks pertinent questions. Does the house have a water closet for the sole use of its inmates? Is it properly flushed with water? If not, how many (a) houses and (b) persons use the same water closet? Is there a properly constructed dustbin or ash-pit for the sole use of inmates? Is the kitchen or scullery fitted with a proper sink? Further questions probe the number of rooms and weekly rent and whether the supply of cottages in a given town is equal to demand.

Clauses of the act applying to sanitary closets and drains are explained. If a house is without a water closet or privy, furnished with proper doors and coverings, the local authority has a duty to require such by written notice. Urban authorities are given powers to make by-laws relating to closets, ash-pits and so on and can close off buildings or parts of buildings unfit for human habitation. If it appears to a medical officer of health or any two medical practitioners that a house is in a filthy and verminous condition, whitewashing, cleansing or purifying can be specified and the owners required to pay.

Campaigner and founder of The National Trust, Octavia Hill, also challenged the Victorian status quo, pioneering the development of social housing and social work. She was the granddaughter of Thomas Southwood-Smith, a contemporary and friend of Edwin Chadwick, and a campaigner for better living conditions for the poor. Hill saw how the Victorian laissez-faire system was failing the poorest members of the working classes, the unskilled labourers. In 1864, she became a landlord of houses in Paradise Place, Marylebone, an area known as "little hell", with her then-friend, the art critic and social commentator, John Ruskin.

Ruskin established the scheme on the basis that investors received a five per cent annual return, any excess being reinvested in the housing. Known as "five per cent philanthropy", this was the concept adopted by other charitable Victorian housing providers, such as the Guinness, Peabody and Samuel Lewis trusts, which created, from the 1860s, blocks of tenement flats (many of which are still in use) in cleared areas of London's slums.

Hill disapproved of the trusts, feeling that they provided an impersonal, overly bureaucratic service and allowed their tenants to take too many liberties. In addition, she favoured traditional house styles, including cottages, with doors opening onto streets, rather than the barrack-like blocks created by the early social housing providers. Later, she would use the same arguments against the provision of council housing, to which she was strongly opposed. Her arguments would find a strong echo a century later, when community organisations campaigned against streets being knocked down, breaking up strong, existing communities, and replaced by tower blocks.

Hill's property portfolio increased. In 1887, she built the Red Cross Garden scheme in Southwark and she developed and managed a large estate for the Ecclesiastical Commissioners in Walworth, also in south London. All her schemes shared the same philosophy. She was concerned that tenants should have access to open spaces and both property and tenants were closely managed, with scrupulous weekly visits for rent collection carried out. By the end of the 19th century, her women volunteer rent collectors, one of whom was a sister of Beatrice Webb, had become paid employees. It was partly because of Hill's example and influence and partly because the First World War removed men from the scene, encouraging female emancipation, that housing management became a professional sphere for the middle-class Edwardian woman – in 1916, an Association of Women Housing Workers was set up.

Pioneering: Red Cross Garden scheme developed by Octavia Hill

However, as in public health (see chapter four) males resented the encroachment of females into their domain. Male-dominated professional bodies would re-assert themselves as the twentieth-century progressed, so that the contribution of women and their associations in the Edwardian period came to be regarded as an anomaly. In a reference to Hill's undoubted influence on the development of a systemised housing profession, the headquarters of the Chartered Institute of Housing is today called Octavia House.

As the 19th century closed, the tide was turning against the charitable and philanthropic housing provider. The 1885 Royal Commission on Housing of the Working Classes exposed deplorable and exploitative housing conditions for the poor, paving the way for strong state intervention. Its findings contributed to the passing of a milestone in the improvement of public health, the monumental Housing of the Working Classes Act 1890.

A clause in the act said that four or more householders could compel by written complaint a medical officer of health to inspect houses considered unfit for human habitation and report that inspection to the local authority. The act empowered local authorities to compulsorily purchase and clear buildings from insanitary urban areas and provide a layout for new housing, following representation by a medical officer of health or 12 rate-payers to two magistrates. It also gave powers for closing and demolishing houses unfit for human habitation and required the sanitary authorities to investigate their local housing conditions.

There was no still no state funding, and there was an expectation that private house builders and philanthropists would build new homes. Local authorities arranged for overall planning, drainage and running water, as well as the removal of waste and ash, but replacement housing was frequently too expensive for the displaced and those who lost their homes may have ended up worst off than before, as wealthier communities moved in instead. Today we would call this process "gentrification". The act did, however, provide an incentive for pioneering local authorities to intervene in poor housing conditions. Many local authorities were surprising progressive in their building endeavours, including London, Birmingham, Manchester, Sheffield, Sunderland and Southampton.

Despite a continuing lack of financial support from the state, the new London County Council, established in 1889, began demolishing slums and building new homes using powers contained in the act. The vestry of Shoreditch in Hackney is said to have built the LCCs first public housing, in 1900, providing disinfectant and delousing facilities for its new tenants. Between 1890 and 1914, the LCC built almost 10,000 units, mainly for those in regular employment, including the Boundary Street Scheme at Bethnal Green, the largest, replacing 15 acres of "awful slums". The new scheme included tenements, shops, workshops, public gardens, a public laundry, baths and club-rooms, provided for little more than the previous the slum rents.

The act led to almost 10,000 council units in London and 3,000 in Liverpool – far too few to meet need, and generally excluding the very poor who remained trapped in poor and insecure housing conditions.

Manchester's new 1890s homes were in Sanitation Street. Some letters were later removed, changing the name to Anita Street, which was felt to be more palatable. Here, new council homes provided sinks, WCs and communal laundries. But, as with some similar schemes, rents proved too expensive for the very poor. The housing was only available to the more respectable working classes who could demonstrate "moral and financial stability".

Not all local authorities were eager to use their new powers to build homes for the working classes: in Leek, Staffordshire, many families were stuck in one room in older slum areas making up a tenth of the town. But the local authority was reluctant to act, anticipating action by individual builders and philanthropic trusts. In 1901, a local man, James Cornes, demonstrated that it was possible, through careful design and construction, to develop new homes for relatively low rents. Even so, the rents, set at 5s to 6s per week, were out of the reach of many who remained in poorer housing, paying around 3s.

In 1902, another wealthy Quaker and chocolate maker, Joseph Rowntree, was influenced by his son Seebohm's study of poverty in York and the emerging garden city movement (see chapters two and six) to create another model workers' settlement, New Earswick. The street layout and house designs were provided by the idealistic and socially-concerned arts and crafts architects Sir Raymond Unwin and Barry Parker (also discussed in the next chapter). New Earswick contains mainly three-bedroom homes, with kitchens and parlours that are designed to catch light. It is still an attractive and popular place to live.

Many people had no option but to remain in Victorian terraces that were over-crowded, lacking in amenities and in a state of substantial disrepair, until long after the Second World War. The worst of these were replaced in post-war slum clearance schemes, but some of the replacement modernist architecture wasn't particularly hospitable, displacing communities and creating, in some people's eyes, "new slums".

I n the Edwardian era, how did it feel to be stuck in poor, privately rented housing, struggling to pay the rent even when in work (there was no housing benefit) and without much hope that anything would change in the foreseeable future? The author Robert Tressell provides us with an interesting and vivid perspective in his 1906 novel, The Ragged Trousered Philanthropists.

In his book he presents the ragged trousered classes – rather than those properly suited and booted – as society's most generous bene-factors, pointing out that they are in fact the people who continually, not always knowingly, give away the financial fruits of their labour to those better off than themselves, their employers and their land-lords. They are forced to live in poverty, suffering poor housing and working conditions.

Tressell's novel, which is said to be based on real people and events, gives us shocking details of the grim housing conditions and powerlessness suffered by the Edwardian working classes. When life got too hard and money too tight (for example, because of illness or unemployment), a "moonlight flit", with one's possessions packed into a handcart, was often the only solution. This would be followed by an insecure tenancy in another inadequate property. Many of the improvements made for private renters after World War Two have now been reversed, so that, in some ways, little has changed.

Born in 1870 in Dublin, Tressell (born Croker or possibly Noonan) moved to South Africa, working as a painter and decorator. He moved to Hastings on England's south coast in around 1899 as a sign writer on lower wages and poorer conditions than he had been used to. He was well educated and radically politically conscious. He had been influenced, like many others, by William Morris, joining the Social Democratic Federation in 1906.

He lost his job, his health deteriorated and he developed tuber-culosis. That was when he began writing The Ragged Trousered Philanthropists, drawing from his own experience as a painter and decorator in Hastings. The unique book combines social realism, in the style of Zola or Dickens, with an explicit Marxist critique of contemporary society in a narrative that is, by turns, heart-breaking, poignant and hilarious.

Ironically, but not really surprisingly, Tressell died from tuberculosis before it was published – the fate of many of his contemporaries enduring insecure employment, low wages, inadequate diet, constant stress and poor housing. He was buried in an unmarked pauper's grave in Liverpool. The book's cause was taken up by his daughter Kathleen but it would be decades before Tressell achieved due recognition – an unabridged version (the original publishers had added a happy ending) was not published until 1955.

The novel describes, beautifully, complex social and environmental determinants of health and the powerlessness of Edwardian working-class tenants. "The Newmans lived in a small house, the rent of which was six shillings per week and taxes. To reach the house one had to go down a dark and narrow passage between two shops, the housing being in a kind of well, surrounded by high walls of the back parts of larger buildings… The air did not circulate very freely in this place, and the rays of sun never reached it. In the summer the atmosphere was very close and foul with the various odours which came from the back yards of adjoining buildings, and in the winter it was dark and damp and gloomy, a culture ground for bacteria and microbes. The majority of those who profess to be desirous of preventing and curing the disease called consumption must be either hypocrites or fools, for they ridicule any suggestion that it is necessary first to cure and prevent the poverty that compels badly clothed and half-starved human beings to sleep in such dens as this."

A century after Tressell's death in 2010, the Labour politician, Tony Benn, wrote a tribute that serves as a pertinent summary and rallying call for modern environmental health practitioners who are concerned with housing conditions. He said: "Robert Tressell… is addressing us with arguments that are just as relevant now as they were when he first used them a century ago. If we want to make progress, we have to do it ourselves and believe that it can be done. That is why this book should be read and studied by this generation, for there is no other way. We must do it ourselves or it will never be done."

*Jill Stewart*

# CHAPTER 6

# Planning

*The deathknell to back-to-back houses, insanitary areas and slumdom has been sounded… we are looking forward to a new Utopia – the ideal hygiene city. We are also looking forward to the time when the air of our manufacturing centres will be almost as pure as the air in the suburb, when the dread scourge of phthisis and tuberculosis will be effectively grappled with, throttled, and overthrown, when infant mortality will be practically a thing of the past, when an antidote to the germ of the bacteria for all infectious diseases will have been found, as in smallpox, diphtheria and enteric fever, and, dare I remark, when Sanitary Inspectors throughout the kingdom will receive proper recognition and a just reward for their labours and risks – risks to which no other official, except Medical Officer, is exposed.*

*Robert Lowe, Sanitary Inspector, Rhyl, paper read at meeting of North Wales Centre, Rhyl, The Sanitary Journal, March 1911*

O n Saturday 7th October, 1905, 150 sanitary inspectors and their friends gathered at the world's first garden city – Letchworth in Hertfordshire. After tea, at 5 pm, they cleared away the tables to hold a meeting. Rapid urbanisation since the Industrial Revolution had caused a major social and environmental impact on increasingly overcrowded and polluted cities, providing Edwardian sanitary inspectors with a busy workload. Their visit to Letchworth was to provide insight into how things might be in the future: better housing, more space, a new relationship between town and country. A better environment – indeed, a new civilisation.

Tea concluded, A. E. Stark, clerk of works, read a topical paper on The Importance of Building Cheap, Healthy Cottages. He mused that he was familiar with the sanitary inspector's role, but felt that instead, a new name, that of health officer or even guardian of health, may be more appropriate and inspire greater confidence. Such a designation, he argued, would promote more input into planning houses; such men would be worthy of higher pay and greater power.

Modern: Letchworth Garden City was designed to be a healthy settlement

Progressively, houses were being improved, he continued – rooms higher, roofs stronger, sanitary appliances and drainage more perfect. But, he cautioned, this all added to the cost and workmen found it impossible to pay high rents. Houses must be adapted to men's means, he continued. This would require both cheap land and cheap housing. Garden cities, he suggested, had done more to meet current demand than any other authority in the country, with no more than 10 cottages per acre helping to secure good road layouts and space around every dwelling.

He went on to say that a healthy cottage should have a good living room, a scullery with a copper, a small fire-grate, a larder not at risk of contamination by bad air, a water closet and three bedrooms, all of which should be well lit and ventilated. He calculated that country labourers had a rent-paying capacity of 2s per week and town labourers 4s per week. Working from this, it would be necessary to provide country cottages at £120 and urban cottages at £150. But securing adequate rents to repay investors would be tricky. Stark implored local authorities to take a flexible approach, within the context of their by-laws, to low-income earners, applying due consideration to design and building techniques, suggesting that concrete could be a durable, useful material. He completed his paper and, after a vote of thanks, the enjoyable meeting was closed.

But what were garden cities, and why was the arts and crafts movement so influential in their development? The arts and crafts movement, the main period of influence of which was from the 1880s to the 1920s, was utopian. It was a response to the Industrial Revolution's mass production, its pollution, horrors and ugliness. The movement sought to reverse a perceived decline in craftsmanship, education and the environment, involved an appreciation of national and local conditions, and promoted the use of local materials and improving the work-life balance – all aspects of what we might now describe as "sustainable development". While its philosophies and ideals were worthy, the movement's aesthetic style struggled to become mainstream, because it was too expensive and remained out of reach for most. Many pioneers of the movement, and some of their clients, were exceptionally wealthy.

John Ruskin, a leading advocate of the arts and crafts movement, funded a range of philanthropic activities including, as we saw in the last chapter, backing Octavia Hill in her first housing scheme in London. His vision included beautiful houses set in small groups in designated areas, providing clean streets, fresh air and views of the horizon. Ruskin's followers would have defined the pillars of the arts and crafts movement as design unity, joy in labour, individualism and regionalism. While these principles did not address the challenge posed by A. E. Stark – that of providing low-cost housing of a decent standard for low-income groups – some arts-and-crafts practitioners did attempt to put social ideals into practice, combining housing, planning and health in their thinking.

Paramount amongst them was the founder of the garden-city movement, Sir Ebenezer Howard. Born in London in 1850, the son of a shopkeeper, Howard emigrated to the USA in 1871. Here, influenced by the writer and philosopher Ralph Waldo Emerson, he became concerned with the quality of life, and set his mind to where people should live and how they could live harmoniously with nature. In 1898, back in England, he published Tomorrow: A Peaceful Path to Real Reform, revised and re-titled in 1902 as The Garden Cities of Tomorrow.

Using the analogy of three magnets, Howard proposed that a garden city would combine the opportunities offered by cities (such as paid work and leisure) with the benefits of country living (fresh

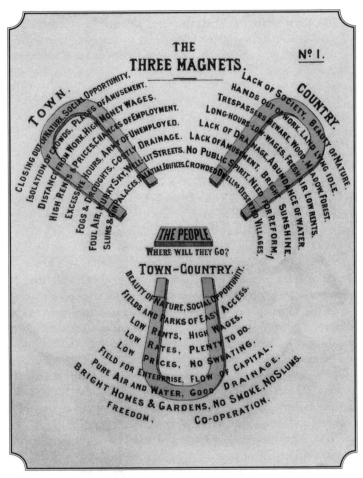

Three magnets: Howard's ideal garden city combined town and country

air, beauty, low rent). The inhabitants of garden cities would enjoy regular employment and decent salaries and live in healthy surroundings alongside manufacturers, professionals and co-operative societies, as well as agriculturalists, who would find new and local markets for their produce. He said of garden cities: "[Their] object is, in short, to raise the standard of health and comfort of all true workers of whatever grade, the means by which these objects are to be achieved being a healthy, natural, and economic combination of town and country life, and this on land owned by the municipality."

These new settlements, he argued, should be of restricted size, carefully planned and surrounded by green belt. They would be independent and managed by those with an economic interest in them, financed by ground rents, with land owned by trustees and leased to citizens. In 1899, Howard founded the Garden Cities Association (now the Town and Country Planning Association).

Following national conferences at Bournville in 1901 and Port Sunlight in 1902 (see chapter five), a company, First Garden City Ltd, was registered in 1903 and a site was chosen for Howard's experiment – Letchworth in Hertfordshire. The timing was right. Land was available to buy, it was near a railway and it was surrounded by agricultural land – perfect conditions for the first garden city. Letchworth, Howard proposed, would represent a "joyous union" of town and country. A design competition was held. It was won by the architects, Sir Raymond Unwin and his brother-in-law and second cousin Barry Parker. They had just designed a model village near York, New Earswick, for Joseph and Seebohm Rowntree (see chapter five).

Both were socialists and followers of the arts and crafts ideals of John Ruskin and the Pre-Raphaelite designer, William Morris. After a private education in Oxford, Unwin, who was born in 1863 in Rotherham, had worked as an engineer at the Stavely Iron and Coal Company's foundries in Chesterfield (a formidably ugly example of industrialisation). Crucially, both Unwin and Parker were committed to providing working-class housing. Their names crop up in connection with almost every garden city and suburb, and, as we shall see, Unwin had a significant influence on government policy after World War One as a senior civil servant.

In a Fabian Society tract published in 1902, Cottage Plans and Common Sense, Unwin and Parker outline a paradigm for healthy living – an antithesis to the foetid and overcrowded domestic environments of the Edwardian poor. They write: "The first consideration in planning any cottage should be to provide a roomy, convenient, and comfortable living room, having a sunny aspect and a cheerful outlook. In it there should be place to breathe freely, room to move freely, convenience for work, and comfort for rest. It must contain the cooking stove, some good cupboards, and a working dresser in a light and convenient place... That nothing can be spent on the ornamentation of an artisan's cottages is no excuse whatever for their being ugly. Plain and simple they may be, but a plain and simple building well designed may be very far from ugly."

With foresight, they add: "A bathroom for every cottage is an ideal which some day will surely come to be regarded as essential." Shared facilities, such as laundries and baths, are emphasised to forge community spirit and help keep down costs for individual families. In line with Parker and Unwin's ideals, a Cheap Cottages Exhibition was held in Letchworth in 1905, sponsored by the Daily Mail and attracting 60,000 people. Letchworth now had its own railway station. The visitors saw well-grouped, generously-sized houses with – an innovation – front and back gardens and to admire the very latest building techniques, including prefabrication.

Amongst the novel exhibits were "vermin-proof walling" and, from the Patent Adjustable Bath Co., the "Cottage Bath of the Century", an appliance equally at home in the kitchen or scullery. Its makers stated: "These baths are largely used in Cottage Property, and when there is no fixed tap over the bath, no extra water rate should be charged. We supply plug, clips and outlet fitting with each bath. Our baths are made of lead-coated steel sheets and will not break like cheap cast iron." A second Cheap Cottages Exhibition was held in 1907, influencing the Daily Mail's first Ideal Home Exhibition in 1908, which was held in the Olympia exhibition centre in London. The event ran throughout the 20th century.

Innovative and worthy of admiration at the time, Letchworth's road plans and house styles were to become visually familiar as the 20th century progressed. The privately-built suburbs of the 1920s and 1930s were undoubtedly influenced by its arts and craft house design; in terms of its scale and vision, it was a precursor for the ambitious council estates conceived by local authority planners and architects after both world wars. It also provided a template, or at least a starting off point, for two phases of new towns – between the world wars (Welwyn Garden City) and after World War Two (Harlow, Stevenage, Skelmersdale, Milton Keynes). The first garden city's creators could not have envisaged that the terms "planning" and "new town" would become terms of ridicule, their utopian dreams buried beneath ugly houses, barren shopping centres and monotonous roundabouts. Aesthetically and socially, what they created in Letchworth was durable and a success.

Great attempts were made in Letchworth to provide three-bedroom cottages as economically as possible. Set out in 1909 and built in 1911 by Bennett and Bidwell for Letchworth Cottages and Buildings Ltd, the Rushby Mead properties were some of the best and provided models for later houses. They were later taken over by Howard Cottage Society Ltd. But it was not just housing that provided the lifeblood to the incoming community – work and leisure were given equal prominence.

As the town developed, with materials brought in by rail, lots of new and relocated jobs were created, for example, for unemployed road builders from London. Letchworth soon attracted engineering, woodworking, printing, publishing and motor companies. Social enterprises were encouraged, including Garden City Co-operators Ltd in 1907, which expanded into a large retail business. Many of the new companies were progressive employers. The Edmonsbury Weaving Works relocated to Letchworth in 1908 – Unwin designed a factory. The company was one of the first to offer two weeks' paid holiday for its employees.

In 1910, the Spirella Company – which patented spiral-wound springs as corset stiffeners – moved to Letchworth. The founder, William Wallace Kincaid, had been impressed by garden city ideals. Spirella came to embody the spirit of the place. It provided a subsidised canteen, a library and bathing facilities for its largely female workforce. The "Spirella Girls" became famous for their formation dancing in the Spirella Ballroom.

Town facilities encouraged communal activities – a picture palace, a skittles alley, tennis courts and a hall for The Church Lads Brigade and Girls Club. Howard, Unwin and Parker often visited the town to enjoy the fruits of their labours. They can be seen in quite a few historic photographs, for example at a Whitsun tour of the estate in 1904, an agricultural conference in 1905 and May Day celebrations.

Mervyn Miller, an expert on garden cities, observes: "The pioneer lifestyle, particularly of the free-thinking vegetarian middle classes, who rejected alcohol, and wore smocks and sandals, became the subject for satire, both locally and nationally." In 1909, Louis Weirter, a local artist, produced a cartoon satirising the Letchworth spirit. The caption reads: "Two German ladies, who visited Letchworth last week, said on leaving: 'We are awfully disappointed in one thing: we were assured before coming that the people at Garden City were only half clothed, and that they all went bare-headed and wore sandals, and we have not seen one person of that sort!'"

Garden suburbs were to be the logical progression from the garden city movement. Dame Henrietta Barnett, a social reformer and author born to a wealthy family in 1851, was horrified by the threat posed to Hampstead of a tube extension, predicting, the increasing numbers of commuters would lead to the "ruin of the sylvan restfulness of that portion of the most beautiful space around London". From the 1870s, Barnett, who was influenced by the theories of her friend Octavia Hill and the garden-city movement, had worked to bring spiritual, moral and social enlightenment to the poor of Whitechapel in the East End, some of London's worst slums, escaping at the weekend to her retreat next to Hampstead Heath.

She tried to purchase part of the heath but was sent away – she was only a woman after all. To increase her credibility, she had to recruit men of influence. That she did. In 1906, she founded a company, Hampstead Garden Suburb Trust Ltd. Its perhaps naïve or unrealistic aspiration was to provide a beautiful and healthy living environment "for all classes". The trust purchased land from Eton College. The Hampstead Garden Suburb Act 1906 helped it to overcome rigid planning by-laws so that the spacious, fluid planning style of the garden city could be replicated in an urban setting. To lend the suburb an arts and crafts feel, Barnett employed Raymond Unwin as planner, and Edward Lutyens and Mackay Hugh Ballie-Scott as architects. The houses in Hampstead Garden Suburb, however, were only to be available to the affluent. Costs ranged from £435 to £3,500 – substantially more than at Letchworth.

Elsewhere in west London, posters went up in 1906 advertising Ealing Tenants Ltd, a society registered under the Industrial and Provident Societies' Acts. The posters invited inspection of the "Brentham Experiment", a garden suburb to be built, in contrast to Hampstead, along co-operative principles. In 1897, Henry Vivian, a carpenter and trade unionist, later to become a Liberal MP, set up a co-operative company called General Builders Ltd, aiming to buy land and to provide its members with work and accommodation. In 1901, he founded, with others, Ealing Tenants Ltd to act as a management body.

By 1905, 50 houses had been completed. The first houses were terraced villas, but that changed in 1907 when Ealing Tenants Ltd purchased more land, and Raymond Unwin and Barry Parker were engaged to advise on house design and layout. As in Letchworth, tenants benefitted from good communal facilities and low housing densities. They paid rents of between 6s 6d and 21s a week and enjoyed dances, whist drives, concerts, lectures, flower shows and pageants. Today, Brentham is a conservation area and has its own website. It has a strong sense of community and the tradition of May Day celebrations is still observed – but the houses are no longer for rent and they are not cheap.

Others followed the garden suburb route. In 1910, work began on Liverpool's garden suburb at Wavertree, and, in 1912, the Flower Estate at Winebank in Sheffield. Planning was becoming important. The Housing and Town Planning Act 1909 prevented the further building of back-to back houses and gave more enforcement powers to sanitary inspectors; by prescribing standards for dwelling layout and density, it ushered in a new discipline and profession – what would later become known as town planning.

Slum-clearance, house-building and planning, all contributors to public health, would become imperatives after the First World War, which increased social expectations and accelerated the pace of change. Raymond Unwin was to be heavily involved. In 1915, he was seconded from the Local Government Board, the body that ran local government, to join the dynamic new Ministry of Munitions as its director of housing. In this capacity, he designed housing for munitions workers in the villages of Gretna and Eastriggs, just across the Scottish border. Although constructed economically, these and other munitions estates were designed to include good landscaping and effective internal layouts.

London-born arts and crafts architect Frank Baines was also influential in the rapid housing programme for munitions workers.

Well Hall garden suburb, or the Progress Estate, which he designed, was begun in 1915 close to the Woolwich Arsenal. It has short symmetrical terraces of four to six houses in a cottage style, all with gardens. The growing transport network was important to its development, and tramlines went to and from the estate to Woolwich. More aesthetically appealing than later council estates, which fell victim to swingeing economies, it is today, like Brentham, a conservation area. It has the familiar arts and crafts hallmarks – well-sized gardens, winding pavements and variegated house designs, featuring generous gables and dormer windows. By a strange twist of fate – perhaps Merrie England was not that peaceful – the estate is where the black London teenager Stephen Lawrence was murdered in 1993.

Arts and crafts architecture: south-east London's Well Hall garden suburb

The progressive wartime government set up, in 1917, a Housing (Building Construction) Committee under Sir John Tudor Walters to investigate house-building and living conditions for the working classes in England, Wales and Scotland. The Tudor Walters committee, the members of which included Raymond Unwin, reported in 1919. It proposed a programme of satellite towns rather than isolated garden cities. It recommended a maximum of 12 houses to the acre in towns and houses with wider frontages than the typical by-law designs of the industrial towns. These principles were included in a detailed manual on state-aided housing issued in 1919. In the same year, a new Housing and Town Planning Act recognised that private enterprise alone would not be adequate to finance working-class housing. Public money would be required through rates and taxation. Now council houses could be built in large numbers. The legislation became known as the Addison Act, after the health minister, Christopher Addison.

Born to a wealthy farming factory in Lincolnshire, Addison was both a medical doctor and politician. Concerned by the plight of the poor, he was elected as a Liberal MP for Hoxton in the 1910 general election. (A long political career, including both world wars, would later see him switch to the Labour party. He served Clement Attlee as the leader of the House of Lords from 1937, as Baron Addison). During the First World War, he was appointed parliamentary secretary to the new Ministry of Munitions by coalition Prime Minister David Lloyd George. Addison became associated with an interventionist programme known as "war socialism", which was designed to speed up armaments production, including the rapid production of the munitions estates. After the war, he was tasked with converting the Local Government Board into a health ministry. And, as the country's first health minister, he was responsible for implementing the act that bore his name. Raymond Unwin, with whom he had worked at the Ministry of Munitions, was his right-hand man – the Ministry of Health's chief architect.

Addison lost his seat in 1922. By then, he was disillusioned that cuts were already being made to Lloyd George's "homes fit for heroes" mass-housing programme, its idealism watered down by political expediency. To his disappointment, meanly proportioned council homes, with outside WCs, no parlours and no living rooms, were still being built.

In his illuminating 1922 book, The Betrayal of the Slums, he writes: "For years past, thinking and patriotic people of all parties have been seriously disquieted by the fact that in England and Wales alone there are nearly a million dwelling places — so-called homes — which consist of not more than two rooms. People are compelled to live in them, because no other habitations are available. In these places, as well as in vast numbers of others which contain more than two rooms, the processes of deterioration are necessarily and rapid.

"Homes of this kind are a perpetual hindrance throughout life to the people who have to live in them. They allow no privacy, afford little or no quiet or rest, even for the child, they give no opportunity for the mind and provide a continual poison for the body. The physical consequences are disastrous to the inhabitants and involve costly burdens on the rest of the community."

Despite Addison's doubts, the enthusiasm and idealism of the Edwardian pioneers of garden cities and social housing, tinged with their arts and crafts aspirations to bring space and beauty to the poor, had been hugely important. Tens of thousands of houses had been built for people on low incomes, homes that were far superior to their rural and urban predecessors; a system had been devised for spatially separating homes from sources of gross pollution and, less glamorously, the daily work of sanitary inspectors had fought against the derelictions and abuses of slum landlords, lengthening the lives of many. For a few decades, revolution had been in the air. That the utopian ambitions of the pioneers – a form of British Bolshevism – did not create a "new civilisation" was not their fault. In fact, Britain's slow and uneven progress in improving its housing was part of larger pattern – a pattern that is still evident.

As Pat Garside reflects, in her introduction to Built to Last?, "The significance of poor housing for ill-health has been recognised by public health reformers since the early 19th century... Yet in significant respects, government intervention has been reluctant, spasmodic and weak compared to other areas of public health."

*Jill Stewart and Jim Stewart*

## CHAPTER 7

# Food

*There has been too much jerry-building, not only of housing but of human bodies; jerry-building by unsound and adulterated food and the supervision which under the Public Health Act you maintain over meat, poultry, game, fish, fruit, milk and other articles prevents widespread poisoning, insidious interference with growth and impairment of health.*

*Sir James Crichton-Browne,*
*The Sanitary Journal, February 1911*

Edward VII, Britain's monarch from 1901 to 1910, was a noted gastronome. It is said that no food was too rich for him. At least four meals a day and dinners of 12 or 14 courses were the norm and he enjoyed each one. Pheasant stuffed with truffles, quails filled with foie gras, sole poached in Chablis garnished with oysters and prawns, boned snipe with Madeira sauce – all were grist to the mill. Edward, whose premature death was hastened by his gluttony and fondness for smoking, would have a cold chicken placed at his bedside in case he became hungry during the night. Such a sugary, alcohol-laden diet – courses were washed down with sherry, hock, claret, champagne, port and liqueurs – often gave rise to digestive ailments in the Edwardian leisured classes.

But what of one of the king's less affluent subjects? An Australian-born journalist and feminist, Magdalene Reeves, researched typical family expenditure and diet in south London in 1911, the year that Edward died. The result, Family Life on a Pound a Week, was published as a pamphlet for the Fabian's Women's Group.

Miss Reeves breaks down the 10s that were spent by a city ware-house worker, Mr W, and his wife every week on food. At 3s, meat made up the largest part of the budget. Then, in descending order, came bread, butter, flour, milk, tea, moist sugar, dripping, potatoes and greens. She writes: "Cold meat, with bread and butter and tea, would be provided for the evening meal." The "eternal bread, butter and tea" would be breakfast.

This budget equates to a not-impossible but spartan and precarious lifestyle. It means scrimping and saving to pay for sickness and burial insurance, and for the endless demands of gas, coal, fares, soap and washing soda; hoping that the husband's job is not lost, that new arrivals to the family won't be too expensive, and that clothes and shoes won't wear out. Luxuries are miniscule – a little beer and tobacco, and occasional trips to the picture-palace or music hall. With a little more income would come gastronomic luxuries – more expensive cuts of meat and fish for the main family meal, as well as fruit, bottled condiments, jam and Colman's mustard.

What Miss Reeves describes in Family Life on a Pound a Week is the benchmark for those who are living just above the poverty line, in an era when unemployment or unexpected illness could cause a catastrophic decline in fortunes and, in the worst case, a spell in the poorhouse.

From his study of York, Joseph Rowntree also calculated a minimum weekly income of just above a pound, 21s 8d, was necessary to sustain "physical efficiency" for a family of three. In his calculation too, a little more than half would be spent on food. But such an income, he asserts, would only provide a meagre diet, even less varied than that enjoyed by able-bodied paupers in workhouses.

The poverty line diet then largely consisted of cheap cuts of meat (often recycled from Sunday), some stewed greens, white bread, butter and tea. The researches of Joseph Rowntree in York and Charles Booth, in London, found that up to a third of city populations lived below the poverty line. So, in an era before food was generally mass-produced and when, in cities, it was often sourced locally and sold from the pavement, what did the very poorest of Edward's subjects eat?

Jack London's journey into the slums of East London, described in his 1903 account The People of the Abyss, delves into the lifestyles and diets of the inadequately-paid and unemployed – families crammed into squalid, overcrowded houses, maimed and itinerant workers reliant upon coffee houses and doss houses, inmates, and casual users of workhouses. He says: "The poor worker of the East End never knows what it is to eat good, wholesome meat or fruit – he rarely eats meat or fruit at all… the slops and water witcheries of the coffee houses never even approximate to what you or I are accustomed to drink as tea or coffee."

He notes: "I have stood outside a butcher shop and watched a horde of speculative housewives turning over the trimmings and scraps and shreds of beef and mutton – dog-meat in the States. I would not vouch for the clean fingers of the housewives... yet they raked and pawed and scraped the mess about in their anxiety to get the worth of their coppers... All day long this heap of scraps was added to and taken away from, the dust and dirt of the street falling upon it, flies settling upon it, and the dirty fingers turning it over... The costers wheel loads of specked and decaying fruit around in their barrows all day, and very often store it in their one living and sleeping room for the night. There it is exposed to the sickness and disease, the effluvia and vile exhalations of overcrowded and rotten life and next day it is carted about again to be sold."

Jack London is appalled by the overcrowding, grudging welfare, low pay and unsanitary condition of the East End, comparing them unfavourably to what he had experienced as a "hobo" and seaman in America. He shows us a race of under-sized pavement-dwellers – men and women ruined by drink, and malnourished and verminous children deformed by rickets. In The People of the Abyss, London only refers to a sanitary inspector once. He appears unaware that inspectors have powers in relation to food. It is probable that confronted by the daunting poverty of the East End and the multi-farious nature of their duties, they were overwhelmed by the demand for their work.

One can point to ad hoc laws protecting the safety of particular foods for centuries but the first comprehensive legislation appeared from the mid-19th century. Before this, there were few restrictions on what could be added to food in order to preserve, colour or bulk it out – for example, alum or chalk dust were added to flour to make it more white, while copper sulphate was added to pickles, preserves and wine. Nor was the consumer effectively protected before refrigeration from rotten meat, sour milk and rancid butter.

The nation was shocked when 20 people died from poisoning in Bradford, in 1858. A careless street trader, "Humbug Billy", had acci-dentally added arsenic instead of a sugar-substitute called "daft" to a batch of his popular sweets, with disastrous consequences.

Improved microscopes and advances in chemical science allowed a chemist, Arthur Hill Hassall, to carry out Britain's first extensive food-sampling programme. The shocking results and a campaign in the Lancet magazine contributed to the passing of the Food Adulteration Act of 1860. In 1872, the law was strengthened by the addition of sampling officers and public analysts, and in 1875, the Sale of Food and Drugs Act introduced meaningful sanctions for those adding "injurious" substances to food or drugs. At last, the law had teeth.

Building on 1855 legislation, Disraeli's comprehensive Public Health Act in the same year gave powers to medical officers of health, which they could delegate to sanitary inspectors, to prosecute sellers of meat unfit for human consumption and to magistrates to issue search warrants and to condemn unfit meat. It also contained provisions, which were not much used, allowing local authorities to set up public abattoirs. The shocking state of abattoirs was a subject that preoccupied The Sanitary Journal from its inception.

In the Edwardian period, the journal's pages were dominated by two foodstuffs – meat and milk. They were traced through the food chain from the abattoir to the butcher and market stall and from the milking shed to the high street and doorstep. Both had been linked, scientifically, to potentially fatal infectious diseases, including the most feared of all, tuberculosis. But in both cases, as we shall see, legislation and effective enforcement were delayed by the producer interests of the farming lobby.

The compendious Public Health Act of 1875 still dominated the work of the Edwardian sanitary inspector. It ran the gamut of sewers, drains and water supplies, refuse, lodging houses, nuisance, offensive trades, infectious and epidemic disease, and safety in factories and workshops. In the most advanced local authorities – usually urban – the act underpinned a public health service of which food safety was only a part.

In the October 1911 edition of The Sanitary Journal, J. A. Robinson, meat and food inspector for the port city of Bristol advocates a change of emphasis in officers' duties and amendments to the law to reflect advances in science and the increasing sophistication of food crime.

Mr Robinson notes: "Inspectors in the past, I imagine, placed more importance upon sanitary matters than upon securing a wholesome food supply – perhaps because of not being so well conversant with the characteristic of diseased food as with a bad drain... Until every inspector realises this, we shall continue to hear complaints of our ineptitude and such sarcastic references to us as 'joiners', 'plumbers', 'drapers' etc. incapable of forming an opinion of diseased meat."

Mr Robinson had a point. In Britain, powers under the Public Health Act of 1875 for inspectors to seize and condemn unfit meat had been patchily applied. In 1882, a German doctor, Robert Koch, had discovered the tuberculosis bacillus (arguably one of history's most significant medical discoveries) and a series of veterinary congresses had suggested, initially inconclusively, that infected meat and milk could cause tuberculosis in humans. This science was contested by the agricultural lobby and those who clung to the old-fashioned "miasma" theory of disease.

In the UK, the celebrated Glasgow meat case of 1889 threw scientific and enforcement issues in relation to food safety into relief. Glasgow council sanitary inspector Peter Fyfe seized two carcasses showing signs of tuberculosis from an abattoir. The owners of the meat – both butchers – contested their destruction. They were prosecuted by Glasgow City Council for selling unfit meat but pleaded not guilty.

Numerous experts were called to a hotly-contested trial that lasted for four days and attracted national coverage. The defence argued that, as only part of the carcasses was diseased, they should not have been seized; the prosecution argued that science had shown that the presence of the tubercular bacillus in part of an animal would render the whole dangerous. The judge found for Glasgow. Following the case, cities with meat inspectors, like Liverpool, Belfast, Leeds and Newcastle began to seize whole carcasses with localised signs of diseased. Outraged butchers lobbied their MPs and the Board of Agriculture.

At the instigation of the Local Government Board, a Royal Commission was set up to look into tuberculosis in animals and humans. Beginning work in 1890, it dragged on for four years. In a minority report, Professor George Brown complained of the undue influence of the meat trade. He called for a properly regulated system of meat inspection by "persons competent to judge as to the effect and character of the tuberculous deposits". A second Royal Commission was convened, reporting in 1898. It agreed that meat inspectors should be appropriately qualified but, crucially, fudged the contamination issue, not accepting that localised disease could mean mycobacteria in the blood and lymphatic systems.

Abattoirs and butchers did not want more carcasses to be condemned and, if they were, advocated compensation. Farmers objected strongly to a system requiring them to certify their animals were healthy and often denied that infected meat caused tuberculosis – lobbying issues that led, in 1908, to the creation of the National Farmers' Union. Meanwhile, medical officers of health disdained lowly veterinary officers and did not often employ them in their sanitary departments (this was less the case in Scotland). Overworked sanitary inspectors were caught in the middle.

It was only in 1924, following centralised control of the meat trade during the First World War and the creation of a Ministry of Agriculture and Fisheries, that detailed regulations on the condemnation of meat and meat inspection were introduced. How many thousands of Britons had died needlessly in the decades since Koch's momentous discovery?

Called "the white plague", tuberculosis was endemic in Britain's Victorian and Edwardian slums. It killed more people than all other infectious diseases put together. Fresh air regimes mitigated its deadly symptoms but it remained untreatable and a scourge of the poor until the 1940s, when antibiotic treatments became available, milk pasteurisation was widespread and the Bacillus Calmette-Guerin, or BCG, vaccine came into use.

By the early 20th century, in other European countries and the USA, meat hygiene was centrally or regionally enforced, with veterinary science to the fore. In the UK, knowledge of animal pathology was still spread thinly and meat-hygiene enforcement by local authorities was inconsistent or non-existent, particularly in rural districts. An examination for meat inspectors was not introduced until 1899 by the Royal Sanitary Institute. In uninspected abattoirs, which produced raw material for the pies and sausages eaten by the poor, diseased meat could easily enter the food chain.

In The Sanitary Journal of 1911, Mr Robinson welcomes the

creation by the Local Government Board of a Food Department and new regulations covering foreign meat and unsound food but he calls for more powers, particularly for port sanitary authorities. He notes: "Every sanitary inspector should possess a practical knowledge and be able to judge of the characteristics of good and bad food. The detection of diseased meat and the seizure of unsound food of all kinds is one of the most important phases of the sanitary inspector's duty."

Staple food: meat hygiene dominated Edwardian environmental health

Sanitary inspectors may, in many cases, have lacked scientific knowledge. But they developed a keen eye for the tricks of the butchery trade. In the March 1910 issue of The Sanitary Journal, Norwich sanitary inspector Bernard Penny notes: "These gentlemen are past masters in the gentle art of faking and can dress a dead lamb or calf and clean up an old cow or weedy steer in a marvellous manner. What with inflating of veal and lamb and stripping and cleaning of beasts, it often takes very careful inspection to detect anything wrong. One of the commonest forms of cag-mag meat in country districts is wet mutton. This is mutton from a sheep that has gone sick on turnips or swedes."

In rural districts, there were generally few, if any, inspectors in abattoirs and the meat trade was dealt with leniently by magistrates, who often had close connections to farmers. But many city authorities employed specialised teams. In 1911, Manchester's sanitary department, for example, employed 100 staff for a city of 1.5 million. Included among the city's 37 district inspectors were specialists on adulteration, milk and ice cream shops, and food and drugs. The city's annual health report for 1908 shows that 161 tons of unwholesome meat were seized or voluntarily surrendered and destroyed during the year, as well as 138 tons of fish and shellfish, and prodigious quantities, measured in barrels, baskets and boxes, of fruit and vegetables. Officers were active in the pig market, slaughter-houses, the Smithfield fish, fruit and vegetable market, shops, warehouses, cold stores, triperies, and sausage and pie factories. Seizure was made using powers under the 1875 and 1890 Public Health Acts. Tuberculosis and decomposition were the principal causes for the destruction of meat.

Apart from diseased meat and decaying fruit, another insidious cause of disease entered every city, town and village daily: milk. Manchester's energetic and long-serving medical officer of health, James Niven, was explicit on the topic in his memoir published in 1923, Observations on the History of Public Health Effort in Manchester. He writes: "The most important article of food is certainly milk, the more so that it is practically the exclusive food for infants and children under two years of age." Contaminated milk, he says, is associated with sore throat, enteric fever (typhoid), scarlet fever, diphtheria and diarrhoea "not to speak of attacks of tuberculosis in the young which have proved to be due to disease in the cow".

Milk was hugely important to the economy of Edwardian Britain – dairy farmers made up a quarter of the agriculture sector – and it was transported a long way to meet the insatiable demands of cities. London's supply came from as far afield as Derbyshire and Devon.

As well as containing bacteria, milk was often watered down. Edwardian inspectors used the Sale of Food and Drugs Act of 1875 to prosecute in cases of dilution. In addition, the much-used Cowsheds, Dairies and Milkshops Order of 1885 proscribed minimum standards for lighting, ventilation, cleaning and water supplies.

In many cases, they were cleaning the stable after the horse had bolted. Well-informed Edwardian sanitary inspectors knew from well-publicised research that up to a fifth of dairy cows were affected with tuberculosis, around 2 per cent with tuberculosis of the udder. They also knew that a technique had been devised to render milk safe – pasteurisation. It had been demonstrated in 1903 by George Newman, later the Ministry of Health's first chief medical officer. Finally, they were aware that dairy farmers were firmly opposed to pasteurisation being imposed upon them.

This public health issue represented the city versus the country. Numerous private milk and dairy bills designed to improve standards presented by John Burns, the president of the Local Government Board and by cities including Manchester and Leeds were blocked between 1900 and 1914.

Some inspectors and medical officers of health were roused to anger. Peter Fylde, the sanitary inspector who had brought the Glasgow meat case, presents an eloquent and impassioned plea for reform in the July 1910 issue of The Sanitary Journal. He writes: "Who can calculate the mass of human suffering, the numberless army of pale-faced pilgrims in their weary march to the consumptive's grave whose painful progress from birth to death has been caused by a draught of disease-bearing milk?

"Education as to the consumptive's sputum goes on continually, disinfection is constantly carried out for phthisis, overcrowding and dirt are being combated every day; but all the while railway trains and the farmers' milk carts are bringing into our cities and towns their daily draughts of milk of which a solid proportion is open to grave suspicion." He notes the causes as, "the dirty, ill-ventilated byre, the dung-plastered cow, the uncleansed udder, the untidy, improperly clothed milker... These things are known and reiteration of them has become tiresome to the public."

A further Royal Commission in 1907 established that bovine tuberculosis was transmissible to humans. But legislation was still blocked by farming interests, particularly through the Central Chamber of Agriculture.

The left-wing Fabian Society, in a pamphlet published in 1899, had proposed a radical solution – municipalisation of the milk supply (after all, it had proved effective for gas and water). The pamphlet noted that infant mortality was increasing and that tuberculosis was spread by milk. It argued: "Many of our large towns have spent enormous sums of money to provide their citizens with clean water: why should they not also provide them with milk?" In municipal dairies, the pamphlet continued, milk would be produced under strict supervision and in hygienic conditions. The well-reasoned but too radical suggestion was not taken up.

Throughout the 1920s, former health minister and pioneer of social housing legislation Christopher Addison and farmer politician Waldorf Astor pressed for tighter controls through the Pure Food and Health Society of Great Britain. Milk was still unsafe in the 1930s – only 30 per cent of the national product was pasteurised and at least 2,000 people, mainly infants, are estimated to have died each year from bovine TB.

Change was postponed by the Second World War, but, at last, the 1949 Milk (Special Designations) Bill arrived – one of the lesser-known measures of Clement Attlee's post-war Labour government. It required, for the first time, that milk sold to the public be either pasteurised or from herds that were assured to be tuberculin-tested. Edith Summerskill MP, a physician who was a permanent secretary in the Ministry of Food, said that the bill was equal in importance to the National Health Service Act. She asserted: "Pasteurisation has been prevented by ignorance, prejudice and selfishness."

Gleaming milking parlours with stainless steel equipment and staff in spotless white overalls must have appeared, in 1910, like novel glimpses from a distant future. The refrigerator had yet to enter the British household (although frozen meat was now imported and exported). Canned goods and mass-produced sausages still had an aura of mystery about them; households had yet to experience the wonders of instant coffee or custard powder. But there were signs of things to come. The Victorian period had seen a flurry of creativity in the biscuit realm – the Garibaldi (1861), the cream cracker (1885) and the digestive (1892). Britain's addiction to tooth-destroying confectionery was long-established, with specialised shops selling chocolate bars, peanut brittle and a galaxy of boiled sweets, which, with luck, did not contain arsenic.

The Edwardian grocer's shop with its blocks of butter and loaves sold in waxed paper would have contained many products familiar to the modern eye: Fry's and Cadbury's chocolate and cocoa, Marmite, Bovril, Colman's mustard. These "branded" products were made in factories, and distributed by rail and road. They could generally be counted on to be free of microbiological contamination and to be "of the nature, or substance or quality demanded by the purchaser".

Britain had been a pioneer of specialised processes and mass production in food and what today we would call marketing. The six-day London conference of the Sanitary Inspectors' Association in September 1910 ("Another brilliant success", the journal boasts) was designed to give inspectors a glimpse of the most modern, scientifically advanced and enlightened techniques in food production.

On the afternoon of the second day, a group of inspectors embarked upon a field trip to "biscuit town". Entrepreneurs James Peek and George Hender Frean had set up their celebrated company, Peek Frean and Co, in south London in 1857. In 1866, they moved to Clements Road, Bermondsey. Benevolent employers, they provided their staff with medical and dental services, sports, music and drama clubs, and a magazine, The Biscuit Box. For decades, their workers in white aprons spilled out onto the local streets. Their factory, in a densely populated part of London close to the docks, made the air smell sweet. Lines produced included the Garibaldi, the Chocolate Table, the world's first chocolate-coated biscuit, and the Bourbon. In the 1930s, the cocktail age, the company was to innovate with Cheeselets and Twiglets (products that are still available).

The Clements Road factory, which employed up to 4,000 people, closed down in 1989. Today, it remains as a brick hulk, one of numerous abandoned factories in a run-down area of scrap yards and railway arches, its history commemorated by a blue plaque.

The inspectors, many from the provinces, were awed by what they saw. An unnamed writer in The Sanitary Journal notes: "We mount stair after stair, fairly amazed at the extensive nature of the works and the multitudinous operations carried on therein. We are particularly struck by the scrupulous cleanliness everywhere displayed. We inspect the numerous crates of eggs, the egg testing machinery, the milk supply, sugar and flour. The marvellous rapidity owing to the splendid machinery and the division of labour with which a biscuit could be produced excited more than a little marvel... the omnipresence of the biscuit seems assured."

Something even more remarkable was to come on the third day of the conference – a visit to the world's largest margarine factory in Southall. Margarine had been patented by French chemist Hippolyte Mege Mouries in 1869. It was invented in response to a competition run by Emperor Louis Napoleon III to find an inexpensive substitute for butter. The product was initially produced by emulsifying beef fat with skimmed milk; later, vegetable oils were used. A Dane, Otto Mønsted, began producing margarine in 1870 and Denmark became the world's largest manufacturer. Margarine was cheap. It was rapidly adopted by the world's growing urban masses and was called the "poor man's butter".

Dairy farmers in the UK disliked margarine intensely. They resisted its development and sale, just as they successfully blocked the adoption of milk pasteurisation. In 1887, the British Parliament passed a Margarine Act. This specified that names suggestive of butter could not be used for the product. Similar laws in other countries dictated that margarine could not be dyed yellow, making it look like butter.

In 1889, Mønsted set up England's first factory in Godley, Manchester. In 1894, he built an enormous margarine plant near Southall station in west London called Maypole Dairy. A marvel in its day, the plant was served by its own railway sidings and canal. The Maypole Dairy Company developed a grocery chain that sold its own products. It was taken over by the William Lever Company in 1914.

Sanitary inspectors attending the 1910 London conference boarded a special train for Southall. The journal notes: "Extremely pleasant and profitable hour spent in witnessing production of once-despised commodity. Prejudice dies hard but after witnessing all details of manufacture, most devoted adherents of dairy-farm produce must say, 'Almost thou persuadest me to be a margarine man'."

The factory, the journal explains, had 1,000 employees and produced 800 tonnes of margarine a week. Two milk trains arrived each day. The milk was then tested bacteriologically, pasteurised, frozen, placed in souring tanks and churned with oils until it emulsified. Cleanliness was important – the workers' blue and white jackets were washed in the company's own steam laundry – and Otto Mønsted was a generous employer. "Large dining halls and kitchens are provided," the journal explains. "A recreation hall comprising concert hall, billiard room and library is in the course of erection."

At the conclusion of the visit, the sanitary inspectors were given tea. Their hosts provided some plates of bread and butter, and others of bread and margarine. They must have noted that there was some still scepticism among those assembled towards "poor man's butter". Evidently proud of their work, they asked their guests to guess which was which.

*William Hatchett*

# CHAPTER 8

# Mental Health

*Madness, the most solitary of afflictions to those who experience it,
but the most social of maladies to those who observe its effects.*
                                        *Michael MacDonald,*
                        *Mystical Bedlam: madness, anxiety and healing
                                in seventeenth-century England, 1983*

On 13th May 1909, Dr Alfred F. Tredgold rose to his feet at the Mansion House in the heart of the City of London to give a speech that would warn of an imminent social and economic threat facing the nation, a threat of such magnitude that if unchecked would lead to no less than national destruction.

Dr Tredgold chose his words carefully. At the heart of his thesis, he told his audience, were hard facts. Facts that he had painstakingly collected over four years proving that Britain faced the very real danger of national degeneracy.

"In the past more nations have sunk to a position of utter insignificance or have been entirely blotted out of existence as a result of the moral, intellectual, and physical degeneracy of their citizens, than of wars, famine or any other condition," he warned his audience. "It would be well if we English were to ponder these facts, for we are rather too apt to rest upon our oars in contemplation of the glories of our past."

As his words reverberated around the magnificent Mansion House interior, even Dr Tredgold could not have anticipated the impact they would one day have on some of society's most vulnerable. What made this speech so significant was the speaker's eminence. This was no fly-by-night zealot warning of imminent social collapse. This was a well-respected member of the medical establishment, a member of the Royal College of Surgeons and author of *Mental Deficiency*, a book that would become the standard text for the treatment of mental ill health and run to eight editions before his death in 1952. But for the purposes of this talk his audience was most interested in the role Dr Tredgold had played as medical advisor and researcher to the Royal Commission on the Care and Control of the Feeble-Minded. Set up in 1904 to consider how best to deal with mental defectives not certified under existing lunacy laws, one of the commission's first tasks had been to define the various grades of mental deficiency that existed.

The Royal Commission's findings would later become the basis of the Mental Deficiency Act of 1913, defining the terms "idiot", "imbecile", "feeble-minded" and "moral imbecile", as well as making it possible to institutionalise women with illegitimate children who were receiving poor relief.

In order to progress, the commission needed to discover the true scale of mental degeneracy across the nation. There were no records to turn to so they had to find a medical expert willing to enter the underbelly of Edwardian Britain and visit the workhouses, prisons, hospitals, reformatories, inebriate homes, indeed anywhere likely to harbour the mentally unwell, and find out exactly what proportion of these communities were mental defectives. The commissioners selected Dr Tredgold and a Dr William Potts for the task. What these two Royal Commission inspectors discovered terrified them.

Dr Tredgold and Dr Potts chose 16 typical districts, some rural and some urban, to visit. The plan was to account for every mental defective in the chosen districts and then extrapolate the figures to get a national picture. As they visited the institutions and worked with doctors and local authorities to assess numbers at large in the community they began to realise the scale of the problem was far larger than anyone had anticipated.

They reported back to the commission that as of 1 January 1906 there were in England and Wales 8,654 idiots, 25,096 imbeciles and 104,779 feeble-minded children and adults. What had so terrified them was that if you added these figures to the 125,827 insane people already accounted for you reached the alarming conclusion that one in every 130 British citizens was mentally defective.

The investigators found a third of mental defectives were living in workhouses, another third were at large and unprotected from life's vagaries while the remainder were either children at school, inmates in prisons or were in inebriate reformatories or similar institutions. No fewer than 66,000 were considered "urgently in need of provision, either in their own interest or for the public safety".

On the bottom rung of the Royal Commission's categories of mental deficiency were idiots. These were deemed to be so defective from an early age as to be unable to protect themselves from common physical dangers. Next came the imbecile. Although more capable than an idiot and so able to protect themselves, they were not capable of caring for themselves or in the case of children being taught to do so. The adult feeble-minded were next on the rung. They were neither idiots nor imbeciles but for their safety and for that of others required care. Feeble-minded school children were incapable of benefiting from instruction.

And finally there were the moral imbeciles. This group from an early age displayed "some permanent mental defect coupled with strong vicious or criminal propensities on which punishment had little or no effect". Unmarried mothers were included in this category.

Dr Tredgold's observations had revealed that the mentally deficient formed a very considerable proportion, if not the whole, of the social failures and the degenerates of the nation. "They not only contribute nothing to a nation's advance, but by their mere presence they actually impede that advance," he warned.

But the drain on national resources, which was calculated to be between £1,000 and £2,000 over each degenerate's lifetime, was not in Dr Tredgold's view the central problem. What frightened him far more was the rate at which they were reproducing.

He had established from the Registrar General that the average number of children born to each married couple across the whole population was 4.63. What had led Dr Tredgold to give his speech at the Mansion House was his further discovery that for each degenerate who married, reproduction rates rocketed to 7.3. The degenerates of British society, he concluded, were mating with the healthy and "dragging fresh blood into their vortex of disease". The vigour of the nation was being sapped and prevention was the only cure.

"If this alarming propagation is not checked the time must inevitably come, if it has not already come, when our nation will contain a preponderance of citizens lacking in that intellectual and physical vigour which is absolutely essential to progress – nay more, when the tide of retrogression will set in and the nation begin to drift along that course which must inevitably end in national destruction."

Dr Tredgold was telling his Mansion House audience that if

the intellectual and moral resources of the nation were to be saved
then procreation between the mentally ill and the healthy must
be prevented. The solution was eugenics. It was a view shared by
the Royal Commission in its recommendation to set up industrial colonies to which the feeble-minded could be banished thus
removing the temptation to breed that was causing such a dilution
of the national stock.

Dr Tredgold and the commission argued that colony life would
both protect the feeble-minded from those only too willing to
exploit them as well as protecting society from them. The scheme had
the added merit of enabling society to reclaim maintenance costs by
putting inmates to work as well as providing a happier environment
on which the feeble-minded could mix. As Dr Tredgold rose to his
feet at the Mansion House that spring evening he was about to earn
himself an extremely powerful ally.

Having served as a young British officer in South Africa and the
Middle East Winston Churchill had early in his career recognised
the relationship between race and social development. He wrote to
his cousin Ivor Guest in January 1899: "The improvement of the
British breed is my aim in life."

When the Royal Commission on the Care and Control of the
Feeble-Minded was set up by the Conservative Balfour government
in 1904, Churchill was in the process of crossing the floor to join the
Liberals. By the time the commission published its eight volumes
of findings in 1908 in the form of the Radnor Report, Churchill
had been promoted to Asquith's cabinet as president of the Board
of Trade.

In that role, he introduced the first minimum wage and established
labour exchanges to help the unemployed find work. He also helped
to draft the first unemployment assistance legislation in the form
part two of the National Insurance Act 1911. Churchill was acutely
aware of the poverty and despair that existed throughout Britain and
saw in the eugenics movement a solution to these social ills.

He had been so impressed with Dr Tredgold's Mansion House
speech, feeling it to be such an eloquent summation of the perils
facing the nation that he gave a copy to each of his cabinet colleagues
in an attempt to persuade them to adopt the Royal Commission's
recommendations.

When he became Home Secretary in 1910, Churchill wrote to the Prime Minister Herbert Asquith: "The unnatural and increasingly rapid growth of the feeble-minded and insane classes, coupled as it is with a steady restriction among all the thrifty, energetic and superior stocks constitutes a national and race danger which it is impossible to exaggerate."

Eugenics was a social theory that was taking Edwardian society by storm. The term had been first introduced in 1883 by Francis Galton, the half-cousin of Charles Darwin, who had become increasingly interested in the ideas surrounding the Origin of the Species, particularly Darwin's chapter on the breeding of domestic animals. Galton dedicated his life to the ideas of selective breeding with the aim of improving the pedigree and therefore the wellbeing of society as a whole.

It was not until the lobby group, the National Association for the Care of the Feeble-Minded, was set up in 1896, and, in 1907, the Eugenics Education Society that his ideas started to gain general currency. In 1905, it is hard to find references to eugenics in the indices of medical and scientific journals, whereas by 1910 it would have been hard to open a newspaper or attend a meeting where these new ideas were not being discussed.

Given this extraordinary shift in opinion, it is not perhaps surprising that the recommendations of the Radnor Report along with the Mansion House speech given by Dr Tredgold in 1909 are in effect an undisguised eugenicist's manifesto. This is even less surprising when you discover that two of the eight members of the Royal Commission were also members of the eugenics lobby groups.

The eugenics movement did not just focus on the elimination of undesirable characteristics. The flip side of their ideas was to increase the fertility of those with desirable attributes through selective parenthood or positive eugenics. This led to some bizarre ideas including the setting up of stud farms and from the philosopher Bertrand Russell the notion of allocating colour-coded discs or procreation tickets to prevent the dilution of the elite. Anyone wishing to have children with someone holding a different coloured ticket would be punished with a heavy fine.

By the time Churchill had been made Home Secretary he was not only showing great interest in the ideas of eugenics but was also reading the work of a Dr H.C. Sharp of the Indiana Reformatory who had pioneered surgery that meant sterilisation no longer required the ethically sensitive act of castration.

Dr Sharp's booklet, The Sterilisation of Degenerates, had influenced the introduction of the compulsory sterilisation of the mentally unfit along with laws outlawing them marrying, into the US state of Indiana just three years previously. Between 1907 and 1981 more than 65,000 people deemed mentally unwell would be sterilised in the United States.

Taking a thick blue pencil Churchill marked paragraphs of Dr Sharp's pamphlet and instructed his Home Office officials to see what could be done to introduce the "Indiana law" in the UK. Keen to adopt the findings of the Royal Commission, Churchill also worked with his Home Office officials on what would be an early draft of the Mental Deficiency Act 1913.

In a Commons speech in February 1911, Churchill called for new powers that would allow the Home Secretary to force anyone found guilty of a second criminal offence to undergo a medical inquiry. If they were found to be feeble-minded, they could be detained in a labour colony for as long as was necessary. He failed to get his way.

Between 1911 and the passing of the act, debates raged as to which was the more humane approach, sterilisation or segregation. The sterilisers argued that vasectomy and ligature of the fallopian tubes were effective and harmless and much more preferable to the loss of liberty.

Segregationists countered that protection and training could be provided in a well-regulated colony which could also provide its inmates with moral reclamation and spiritual salvation. And there was always the risk that sterilisation would be seen as a licence for promiscuity without consequence, surely a fast track to vice, venereal disease and eternal perdition. It was also argued that sterilisation being irreversible placed an impossible moral burden on both doctors and the judiciary. The segregationists won the day.

It would be a mistake to think that the ideas of the eugenics movement went unopposed. Opposing the bill from the start in the name of liberty, the liberal MP for Newcastle-under-Lyme Josiah

Wedgwood led the charge against what he saw as a eugenicist charter. While he recognised the need for homes for the feeble-minded, he objected to any degree of compulsory detention believing people should be able to chose whether they entered into the state's care.

He also questioned the science behind the bill arguing it proposed to restrict the liberty of up to 150,000 people based on highly dubious scientific definitions of feeble-mindedness. He believed the bill was nothing more than a thinly-veiled attempt to restrict the liberty of the working classes and women.

"The spirit at the back of the bill is not the spirit of charity, or the spirit of the love of mankind. It is the spirit of the horrible Eugenics Society which is setting out to breed up the working classes as though they were cattle," warned Wedgwood.

Social exclusion: inmates of the Horton Asylum in Epsom c1910

Through his dogged opposition, Wedgwood managed to earn some safeguards to protect individual liberty as well as narrowing the number of people that would come under the act to 30,000. Despite this victory, Wedgwood battled on and in a last ditch attempt to thwart its enactment he spent two nights at the end of July 1913 single-handedly proposing amendment after amendment in an attempt to talk the bill out. The bill was finally passed by 180 votes to three.

The 1913 Mental Deficiency Act defined four grades of mental defective: idiot, imbecile, feeble-minded and moral imbecile. To look after these categories of mental defectives local authorities would be expected to set up suitable institutions or colonies with staff to supervise, protect and control as well as to detain all mental defectives in their area coming under the scope of the legislation.

Powers of detention came into play when a mental defective was found to have no means of support, had committed a criminal offence or had been detained in an asylum, industrial school or inebriate reformatory. Any woman in receipt of poor relief when pregnant or while giving birth to an illegitimate child could also be held.

Unfortunately for the drafters of the legislation, it contained an enormous loophole. Local authorities could apply to a central body, The Board of Control, for buildings currently being used by the poor law guardians to be used for the housing of their mental defectives. Given that the purpose of the legislation had been to remove the mentally unfit from the workhouse the board was reluctant to let the local authorities delegate their responsibility back to the guardians, so slowing the whole process down.

The outbreak of the First World War shifted priorities slowing the process even further so that ten years after the act had been passed a third of all detainees were still in the poor law system. The remainder were being looked after in a variety of different institutions including hospitals, philanthropic institutions and training colonies run by local authorities.

To understand why eugenics became the prism through which the Royal Commission approached mental ill health and why eugenicists believed their mission was to save society from imminent collapse it is useful to reflect on the economic and political context of the time.

L and ownership had always been the bedrock of the establishment and yet one of the consequences of British expansion had been to open agriculture up to competition from the colonies and America. Between 1870 and 1910, three million acres of land were taken out of cultivation while agricultural wages fell by a quarter. The introduction of inheritance tax along with the loss of rent from their estates meant the coroneted classes were selling their estates to the nouveau rich who had made their money from the grubby sweat of industry and trade. It is estimated that between 1870 and 1930 almost a quarter of privately owned land went on the market. Old England was dying from its roots up.

At the other end of the spectrum, competition was also hitting industry. Countries that had historically imported coal, textiles and metals were now in competition which meant using machines to cut production costs and cut labour. The result was the birth of an empowered union movement fighting for jobs and better working conditions.

Society was changing and with change comes fear. The London unemployment riots of February 1886 had shown that the casual poor were a real threat to the propertied classes. As the historian Gareth Stedman Jones has argued, the middle classes in the last decades of the 19th century were becoming increasingly alarmed by the political threat posed by the rising numbers of casual labourers. The bulwarks of land ownership, class and status were under siege, allowing the great unwashed into the establishment's citadel, Parliament itself. The Scottish socialist, Keir Hardie, had become an MP for the West Ham South constituency in 1892 and by the 1906 election 29 Labour MPs had seats. There was also the growing feeling that the failure of sanitary reforms, slum clearance and charitable interventions to eliminate this risk was due to the problem being of a biological rather than environmental nature.

The failure to recruit sufficient numbers of fit troops during the second Boer War fed into the notion of national decline. A Royal Commission had found that the army had rejected 60 per cent of young men recruits who were suffering diseases caused by malnutrition, overcrowding, low wages, mental deficiency and contaminated milk supplies. Between 1904 and 1914, there were no fewer than eight Royal Commissions investigating national efficiency and the threat of degeneration.

This provided the perfect political backdrop for the eugenicist lobby. Operating outside party politics, organisations such as National Association for the Care of the Feeble-Minded and the Eugenics Education Society were warning of an immediate threat of degeneration and power loss.

The eugenicists were also arguing that a direct link existed between feeble-mindedness and the overriding social problems of the time: crime, prostitution, poverty, unemployment, alcoholism and juvenile crime. But most importantly they were providing the ideas through which a programme of national regeneration would wrestle old England back from the abyss.

The appeal of eugenics in Edwardian Britain cannot just be put down to a fear of economic and political change. New theories were appearing like those of the German biologist August Weismann's who had found a "germ cell", that controlled development in humans and which could not be modified by disease or injury. This gave supporters of eugenics the scientific evidence they needed to support the view that environmental reforms would only have a limited impact. You can change the living conditions of the poor as much as you like, they argued, but when they have children you have to start all over again because, according to Weismann's research, their dissolute nature is inherited. The Austrian scientist and Augustinian friar, Gregor Mendel, was also validating eugenics through his work on inherited traits in sweet peas. The new science of genetics was feeding into the eugenics movement.

Malthusian ideas concerning the dangerous fertility of the poor were well-developed by the end of the Victorian era. So, too, was the tradition of middle class interventions to ameliorate the lot of the industrial poor through education, temperance and sanitation. These were responses to the growth of an industrial proletariat and sub-proletariat also called the residuum, the pauper class, the social problem group and sometimes even the dangerous class.

While this explains why the Edwardians were gripped by the ideas of Galton it does not explain why they were so preoccupied with the feeble-minded as to set up a Royal Commission the recommendations of which would be manifested in the Mental Deficiency Act of 1913.

Up until the mid to late-1800s, the condition known as feeble-mindedness had been seen as a private matter and not of interest to the state. In the lexicon of mental deficiencies the feeble-minded were not normal and so were unable to cope but were seen as being above idiots and imbeciles. Dickens novels are littered with the feeble-minded and mentally deranged, living life in a state of child-like innocence immune to the harsh vagaries of the real world.

So how does the comic Mr Dick in Dickens's autobiographical novel David Copperfield turn from being an object of pity to becoming one of the major social problems of the age? To understand how this shift takes place we must first look at the move to mass compulsory education started by the passing of the 1870 Education Act.

Known as the Forster Act, after its author the Liberal MP William Forster, the act established local school boards responsible for the elementary education of children aged between five and 12. While it would take another 10 years for compulsory education to be introduced up to the age of 10 and many more years before most children actually got an education, the Forster Act did result in large numbers of poor children being educated for the first time.

This meant that a previously hidden strata of society was coming to the attention of social reformers who were becoming increasingly alarmed about the numbers of children struggling to cope. Previously unnoticed physical and mental problems were emerging.

In 1885, the government set up a Royal Commission on the Blind, the Deaf, the Dumb and Afflicted Classes, which confirmed the fear that large numbers of school children were suffering mental deficiencies.

A further committee set up to investigate the scale of the problem found that out of 50,000 children from the London area 9,186 were either "mentally dull" or showing "visible defects". The research led to the Elementary Education (Defective and Epileptic children) Act 1899, which gave local school authorities the power to set up special schools or classes for children struggling with mental impairment.

Another reason for feeble-mindedness becoming an Edwardian preoccupation was the need for the middle classes to make sense of why they were benefiting from economic growth and yet the casual poor seemed to be growing in numbers while failing to reap any benefits.

Great inequalities of wealth existed in 1900. In the1890s, Charles Booth's Survey of Life and Labour in London had revealed between a third and a quarter of the population lived in abject poverty. A working class family was forced to live on 18s a week whereas a middle class family would spend £10. To make sense of this, the view was formed that years of slum life had created a feeble and tainted underclass incapable of self-improvement.

Social failure was not now just seen as a consequence of immorality and a lack of economic opportunity, but mental deficiency as well. Feeble-mindedness was now the root cause of most of society's ills. Poor educational achievement, poverty, immoral behaviour, prostitution, alcoholism and crime could all now be traced back to this wellspring.

It was for these reasons that voluntary organisations started to lobby parliament to discover the scale of the problem, leading to the 1904 Royal Commission and to the Mental Deficiencies Act. So in retrospect how successful were these attempts? In short, not very.

I n July 1923, at the 91st annual meeting of the British Medial Association in Portsmouth, Mrs Ellen Pinsent, one of the eight commissioners who had sat on the Royal Commission on the Care and Control of the Feeble-Minded and now a commissioner on the Board of Control established under the 1913 Act, outlined the failings of the legislation.

Mrs Pinsent reminded her audience of what the 1913 act had tried to achieve. First it had tried to address the large number of mental defectives living unsupported lives who were causing injury to themselves and others through crime and dissolution. The act also intended to stop the merry-go-round of petty offending by the feeble-minded, which short punitive prison sentences were failing to stop.

It was also hoped that the new sanctuaries would provide a therapeutic refuge for the large numbers of patients languishing in lunatic asylums who no-one had any idea what to do with. Continuity of care for those who needed it, overseen by a central Board of Control, had been the overriding objective of the act.

Sadly, the reality fell far short of the intention. Only 14 local authorities had their own institutions or colonies for the mentally defective while the rest relied on charitable and philanthropic efforts or on the poor law institutions. In addition to financial constraints caused by the war leading to a shortage of beds, the act had failed in its intention to coordinate care.

Under the regime, children up to seven were dealt with under the

Mental Deficiency Act, then, from seven to 16, they were the responsibility of the Board of Education which then failed to inform local authorities on their release. The Home Office was responsible for mental defectives in prisons while the Department of Health dealt with those who came under the poor laws.

"It is still to a large extent true that mentally defective persons pass from one authority or institution to another helped or detained a little in each but permanently cared for by none," Mrs Pinsent told the gathered members of the BMA.

There had also been little success in releasing those trapped in asylums. "The mental hospitals still contain large numbers of congenital cases who could be better dealt with in colonies for the feeble-minded," said Mrs Pinsent. While shortages of suitable accommodation were part of the problem, a lack of cooperation between the mental hospital visiting committees and local authorities meant patients could languish for years in inappropriate institutions.

Another serious obstacle was the ability of medical officers to decide which category, if any, a patient fell into. Wedgwood had, in the end, been proved right. Evelyn Fox, a leader of the Central Association for the Care of the Mentally Defective, a body set up by the Board of Control to support its work, observed: "No hard or fast line can be drawn between the idiot and the imbecile, the imbecile and the feeble-minded, the high grade feeble-minded and the dull, backward or sub-normal individual, nor is it easy to distinguish between the moral imbecile and the immoral, criminal individual of a low mental grade."

The First World War changed attitudes to mental ill health and the science of mental ill health developed a more curative model. Evidence was emerging that inherited mental deficiencies were not so clear-cut. The recognition that the fertility of the feeble-minded had been over-estimated along with changing attitudes towards the causes of poverty heralded an era in which the terminology and arguments of the eugenics movement would eventually become little more than a historical curiosity.

*Stuart Spear*

# CHAPTER 9

# The Workhouse

*Civilisation has increased man's producing power an hundred-fold, and through mismanagement the men of Civilization live worse than the beasts, and have less to eat and wear and protect them from the elements than the savage Innuit in a frigid climate who lives today as he lived in the stone age ten thousand years ago.*

*Jack London, The People of the Abyss, 1903*

On a cold, wet winter's day in 1909, the campaigning journalist Everard Wyrall, posing as an out of work clerk, set out to walk from London to Portsmouth planning to stay in workhouses en route. Wyrall was the latest in a long line of writers and journalists who realised that there existed among the Edwardian and Victorian middle classes a lurid fascination for the workhouse creating a market for social documentary. The illustrated weekly magazines that had sprung up throughout the 19th century saw in the workhouse a rich narrative vein.

Charles Dickens called this the "attraction of repulsion". He would have known, he had in 1837 penned probably the most famous workhouse scene as the nine-year-old Oliver asks for more. Oliver Twist, Dickens's portrait of Victorian poverty, was based on his own experiences of the workhouse. George Eliot, Frances Trollope and Thomas Hardy, along with many more authors would soon follow in his footsteps and use literature to plant a horror of the workhouse into the collective imagination.

Of course, to the third of the population living just one misfortune away from entering its brooding environs the workhouse was far more than a literary device or a source of prurient interest. To them it was the ever-present spectre of all things dreadful in life, a hopeless cycle of indignity, disgrace and hardship, ending with the merciful release of a paupers' grave.

Like all good journalists, Wyrall timed his journey knowing there was a market for his story. The long-awaited report from the government's Royal Commission on the Poor Laws and Relief of Distress had been commissioned in 1905 and published in February 1909. Wyrall anticipated that the pubs, coffee houses and drawing rooms of Edwardian England would be abuzz with talk of the future of the workhouse and poor relief by the time he had chronicled his journey. At the time, according to Poor Law Commission estimates, 930,000 people, or one-in-44 of the population of England and Wales were in receipt of some form of poor relief.

The poor law was seen by most as a failure for differing reasons. Those who supported the view that to cure poverty the workhouse must act as a deterrent complained that many of the boards of guardians, responsible for overseeing the day-to-day running of the workhouse, had become too lenient and had lost sight of the poor law's original intention to make relief uncomfortable. More enlightened observers felt the poor law to be unnecessarily draconian as poverty was not, as commonly believed, due to fecklessness but to do with the vagaries of the economy. Whatever your view, the poor law had become an expensive failure. In the ten years ending in 1905 the average cost of maintaining a pauper had risen by fifty per cent from £9 8s annually to £14 13s.

Unfortunately, by the time the Royal Commission came to publish its findings it also could not agree on what caused poverty. The commissioners divided into two camps producing two reports. The majority report argued the origins of poverty to be moral while the more radical minority report argued they were economic. This thrust debate about poverty centre stage. It would be the minority report, authored by the social campaigners and Fabians Beatrice and Sidney Webb, that would, in the end, have a more lasting impact, inspiring the economist and social reformer William Beveridge to write his 1942 report on Social Insurance and Allied Services which was to become the blueprint for the welfare state. Wyrall's objective was far less ambitious. His aim was to publish a pamphlet entitled The Spike, slang for the casual ward of the workhouse, chronicling his experience to coincide with the commission's findings.

Wyrall soon discovered that the life of the vagrant had changed little in the first decade of the twentieth century. Banned from returning to the same workhouse vagrants were forced to walk from spike to spike, often a day's "tramp" apart, in search of shelter. Early on his journey Wyrall found being endlessly on the move to be the first of his many new found privations.

"By now the water had begun to ooze from my boots," he writes. "The rain had long ago penetrated my thin overcoat, and had commenced a frontal attack on my undercoat. The water trickled down my face. I trudged on, almost worn out, and cold and hungry. Heavens I fancy such a life all the year round!" Things would get far worse for Wyrall once in the workhouse.

What to do about the destitute and poor was a centuries-old problem. Until Henry VIII dissolved the monasteries in the 1530s, the church had provided sanctuary for the poor. The monasteries gone, responsibility fell to wealthy landowners until 1601 when the Poor Relief Act, known as the old poor law, introduced a formal rate of tax for every householder of each parish to provide handouts to the destitute.

By the late 18th century, around one-in-seven parishes had built a workhouse to benefit from the economies of scale offered by housing all the parish paupers under one roof. Despite this, most poor relief was still handed to people outside the workhouse, opening the system up to accusations of abuse. In 1795, the Speenhamland system, introduced mostly in the South East, linked relief to the price of bread. With the end of the Napoleonic wars in 1815 and the introduction of the corn laws the cost of relief soon rocketed.

With rising costs and the poor law's failure to cope with industry's demand for greater labour mobility, change was inevitable. The 1834 Poor Law Amendment Act brought parishes together under new poor law unions. Each union was to have a workhouse of last resort providing living conditions worse than those of the poorest independent worker. Meanwhile out door relief was to be discouraged.

The underlying idea behind the 1834 act was that genuine unemployment of the able-bodied did not exist. Anyone able-bodied entering the workhouse was therefore deemed feckless and idle. The terror of the Victorian workhouse had been born and would remain lodged in the nation's collective imagination until well into the twentieth century.

Between 1834 and 1909, when Wyrall found himself looking for shelter on the road to Portsmouth, improvements had been made to make the lot of those condemned to the workhouse easier. In particular the elderly, young and ill now benefited from more benign regimes, but the overriding feeling that poverty was ultimately a moral failing that deserved punishment still prevailed. And as Wyrall was to discover this was felt most acutely by the vagrant.

Vagrants were not mentioned in the 1834 act. It was not until 1842 that the Poor Law Commission ordered they be given separate accommodation in a casual ward in return for four hours labour before they were released. It was preferable to being caught begging or sleeping in the open which meant a fortnight of hard labour under the Vagrancy Act of 1824.

On his arrival, Wyrall washed in water used by vagrants who had already arrived. He was issued a thin nightshirt and his possessions were removed. After being offered bread he was locked in a cell with a wooden board for a bed.

"The door slammed, the locks clicked loudly, the bolt shot – and I was alone. The cold brick floor sent an icy chill through my body. As I tried to arrange the well-worn blankets to the best advantage I envied the sentenced thief his straw pallet. Thousands feel as I did that night, and in their broken-hearted wretchedness seek in prison that relief which should be given them in the place meant for that purpose — the casual ward." After a fitful night's sleep, Wyrall was presented the bill.

He was shown into a corrugated shed with snow blowing through broken windows and told to smash stones until they could be passed through a sieve. "We literally gasped as the enormity and almost impossibility of the task dawned upon us. The mesh of the sieve was less than a quarter of an inch; some of the stones were at least twelve inches in diameter," he writes. Finding that pounding the stones made little impression Wyrall turns his attention to his wretched neighbour.

"The lame man worked like one demented — smashing, sifting, and piling up the fragments. It was a ghastly task. In his eyes I noticed something suspiciously like a tear, and he often cried out that his back ached. He now and then rubbed his wrinkled face as a sharp chip of stone struck him." His fellow vagrant knew that the price of failing to complete the task was a jail sentence.

Life in the Edwardian workhouse could be undeniably grim.

However over the past 60 years things had much improved making the conditions of more permanent workhouse residents far better than Wyrall's experience.

Diet was an area which had seen marked improvement. In 1835, the purpose of the mealtime was to remind inmates that life inside was far worse than life outside. Bread and a thin porridge or gruel was a typical breakfast. Lunch could be bread, cheese or broth with boiled beef and potatoes maybe twice a week. Bread cheese or broth was once again served for dinner. In contrast, after 1900 workhouses were allowed to create their own weekly menus from around 50 dishes including Irish stew, shepherd's pie, fish pie, dumplings and fruit pudding. Gruel was still a menu option and the workhouse cookbook meant that the same ingredients, recipes and cooking methods were to be used to prepare meals in each workhouse

Segregated: women in the St Pancras Union Workhouse in 1910

Forced segregation had always been seen as a great hardship within the workhouse regime. Children were split from parents and wives from husbands. Even in the dinning hall a cloth was often draped between men, women and children to avoid contact. This seemed cruelest for elderly couples facing their final years alone and in 1847 the Poor Law Board ruled that couples over 60 should be provided their own bedroom if they so desired. Unfortunately, a lack of resources meant that by 1895 only 200 elderly couples shared a workhouse bedroom.

By 1900, boards of guardians were recommending outdoor relief for the elderly where possible. When they remained in the workhouse conditions were relaxed, with flexible eating, sleeping and visiting times along with supplies of tobacco and tea. By the end of the Edwardian period, life in the workhouse for the elderly was, for some, better than life outside.

Advances had also been made in the education of workhouse children. From the start, education was seen as a child's route out of the pauper's life. Workhouse schools were formed in 1834, the first form of state education. By 1844, poor law unions were allowed to provide district schools to educate children away from the workhouse and by the 1870s workhouse guardians were being encouraged to send their wards to local schools set up under the 1870 Education Act, the birth of universal education. By the 1890s, pauper children were starting to be housed in local houses and looked after by married couples appointed by the guardians.

While the workhouse can be seen as the start of state education, it can also be argued it was the beginning of universal health care. Until the 1860s, care was given by pauper inmates and untrained staff. Following pressure from Charles Dickens, Florence Nightingale and the medical journal the Lancet, amongst others, significant improvements in health care were introduced. The 1867 Metropolitan Poor Act meant London unions having to set up hospitals outside their workhouses, many of which outgrew their role of dealing with the destitute. By the 1880s, admission to workhouse infirmaries was allowed to anyone who could not afford medical care. It was the beginning of a state-funded medical service. Later, the National Health Service would inherit the last of the workhouses, then known as Public Assistance Institutions, along with their infirmaries, at its launch in 1948. Some of these hospitals ran tramp wards for the destitute up until the 1960s.

Despite these improvements, the poor law was hated by those dependent on it and distrusted by those who were not. The poor law was once more in need of reform. Expectant mothers were two to three times more likely to lose their babies if born in a workhouse.

Refused outside medical help or midwifery services a mid-1900s study discovered that of the 8,483 babies born into the 450 workhouses who responded to the survey, 1,050 were dead within the year. Life was regimented, work repetitive and families divided.

The decision to set up a Royal Commission to look into the poor law was one of the last acts of Arthur Balfour's Conservative government. The Royal warrant confirming the appointment of the commission was dated 4th December 1905, the same day Balfour resigned. The Liberal leader Henry Campbell-Bannerman took office the following day appointing Lloyd George as President of the Board of Trade and Winston Churchill under-secretary for the colonies. After Campbell-Bannerman's death in 1908, Herbert Asquith took over the Liberal leadership promoting Lloyd George to chancellor and Winston Churchill to the Board of Trade. The result was one of this country's most reforming periods of government.

The Liberals first chose to improve the lot of children. By the end of their term in 1914, they had introduced free meals for children of needy parents, the protection of children deemed at risk, the prosecution of cruel or neglectful parents, the banning of the sale of cigarettes to children under 16, the banning of under-14s from pubs, the setting up of juvenile courts and the registration and inspection of nursing and private children's homes.

The Old Age Pension Act of 1909 introduced a non-contributory state pension for men and women over 70. The scheme paid 5s a week to everyone with an income of less than 8s from other sources. The pension decreased for anyone earning up to 12s, after that you received nothing. There were however many exclusions including anyone who had claimed poor relief within the previous two years, anyone who had been imprisoned within the last 10, if you were a drunkard or if you had habitually failed to find work.

For the 600,000 who qualified for the state pension, withdrawing their money from post offices meant being taken out of the poor law regime and so being removed from the shadow of the workhouse and the stigma of poor relief forever.

But it was the legislation dealing with unemployment where the most profound impact was to be felt. In 1908, Churchill called unemployment the "untrodden field of politics". The unemployment riots in the winters of 1886 and 1887 along with trade depressions of 1892 to 1895, 1903 to 1905 and 1908 to 1909 meant unemployment was seen by many as the route cause of poverty, crime, vagrancy and prostitution.

Trade union agitation to reduce unemployment had found expression in parliament through Labour MPs, while it was becoming clear that even the Royal Commission's more conservative majority report would be recommending unemployment insurance and training for the unemployed. The problem for the Liberals was how to introduce a self-financing system that would be separate from the poor laws and yet include all workers, not just members of trade unions.

Beatrice Webb told Churchill at a lunch she had arranged: "If you are going to deal with unemployment you must have the boy Beveridge." The future architect of the welfare state was dutifully recruited into the Board of Trade to help draft the Labour Exchange Act 1909. By 1914 over 450 exchanges had been set up across England and Wales where, thanks to the 1911 National Insurance Act, the unemployed could sign on to receive 7s a week for up to 15 weeks in any one year. These benefits were an insurance against losing your job, funded by a weekly payment of 2 1/2d each by employers, employees and government.

But before Churchill and Beveridge drafted part II of the National Insurance Act they had to wait for Lloyd George to draft the first part dealing with ill health. This part of the act meant employees had to make a weekly contribution of 4d, employers 3d and the state 2d into a state insurance scheme. The insured could then claim during periods of illness for up to 26 weeks in any year or 5s a week disability allowance and the right to stay in a sanatorium.

Initially, this was an unpopular tax. The fixed rate meant that the less you were paid the greater percentage of your wage you lost. It was seen by many as a straight pay cut and there was no guarantee that you would fall ill and be able to reap the benefits. Thirteen million had, however, signed up by 1913 establishing national insurance as a safety net that exists to this day.

Given this blizzard of reform it is extraordinary that the Liberals had managed to introduce such radical change without amending what had been the mainstay of poverty relief since the 1600s, the poor law. Rather than taking a wrecking ball to the workhouse the Liberals had chosen to chip away at its foundations. It would unfortunately take many more years for the process to be complete. It was the Royal Commission's inability to agree on its own recommendations that allowed the Liberals to side step the poor law by in effect ignoring both the majority and the minority report recommendations.

Another reason for the Liberals circumventing the poor law was that after 1900 the workhouses were beginning to reform themselves. More enlightened boards of guardians increasingly populated by women and the working classes were introducing more humane regimes. Better conditions for the elderly along with the cottage homes for children were part of this process.

Another significant reason for leaving the poor law alone was that both the minority and the majority reports had called for the abolition of the boards of guardians. The Liberals knew what strong vested interests existed within the boards and that it would be politically more expedient to just bypass them all together.

Given the economic and political backdrop of the time, the findings of the Royal Commission should have provided the key to tackling poverty. Its terms of reference set down by Balfour had been to "inquire into the working of the laws relating to the relief of poor persons and into other means for meeting distress arising from a lack employment and to consider whether any changes to the poor laws or new legislation for dealing with distress were advisable."

As it turned out, the country would have to wait until 1929 for the boards of guardians to be abolished and until 1948 for the final death knell to be struck when the National Assistance Act declared: "The existing poor law shall cease to have effect". So how had the Royal Commission managed to so spectacularly neuter itself? Especially given that it had been very thorough during its three years of deliberation with commissioners visiting 200 unions, inspecting 400 institutions, interviewing 450 witnesses and taking 900 written statements. The answer lies in its composition.

The retired Conservative government minister Lord George Hamilton was appointed chair. Amongst the 18 other commissioners were some of the most influential social reformers of the time. In addition to Beatrice Webb, there was housing reformer Octavia Hill and the social scientist Charles Booth. There was also a cross section of representation from trade unions, local government boards, boards of guardians and the church. But there was one group that was represented above all others, the Charity Organisation Society.

Founded in 1869 by Octavia Hill and Helen Bosanquet, who was also appointed to the commission, the COS was a charity that firmly supported the notion of self-help and limited government intervention. Six of its members, including its secretary Charles Stewart Loch, had been appointed to the commission and it was this view that prevailed in the majority report signed by the chair and 14 other commissioners. Beatrice Webb said of the six COS commissioners that they all "began the enquiry as convinced adherents of the principles of 1834".

However, the majority report did have much in it that Beatrice Webb and her three fellow minority report signatories, Labour MP George Lansbury, TUC member Frances Chandler and the London cleric the Reverend Henry Russell Wakefield, could agree with.

They all agreed there was too much duplication between local authorities and the poor law and a general failure to tackle involuntary poverty. They also agreed that the introduction of labour exchanges, the raising of the school leaving age and the decasualisation of labour would all help decrease poverty. There was also agreement that there should be means-tested benefits.

Beatrice Webb and her supporters however disagreed with their fellow commissioners that the boards of guardians should be replaced by aid committees made up of co-opted members from the voluntary sector. The majority wanted the maintenance of the poor law and for the organised voluntary sector to be responsible for dealing with poverty not government.

Beatrice and her co-author Sidney Webb were highly suspicious of the efficacy of the COS and so argued for the more radical break up of the poor law which they believed was based on the flawed premise that destitution was a preventable social disease that could be cured through deterrence.

Poverty, they argued, was highly complex with myriad causes. The unemployed, the sick, the feeble-minded and the elderly all required different approaches to their circumstances that were way beyond the wit of a board of guardians. Responsibility should therefore fall to elected local authorities which would tackle such complex issues through specialist committees, informed by expert scientific knowledge.

Unemployment, however, should be the responsibility of central government. A ministry of labour would be responsible for the able-bodied unemployed, whose circumstances were often due to events beyond their control. Both reports agreed that for the hard core intractable "residuum" who were beyond help a penal system of work camps should be set up.

Under the Webbs' plan, the specialist committees would call on the scientific evidence emerging from a new trend in systematic social surveys that researchers like Charles Booth and Seebohm Rowntree had pioneered (see chapter two). Booth had shocked the country by asserting that most Londoners were living below the poverty line as a consequence of unemployment, short-time working and low pay. After investigating poverty in York, Seebohm Rowntree reported in 1901 that 28 per cent of the city's population was living in "obvious want".

The COS, on the other hand, believed that Beatrice and Sidney Webb's approach failed to acknowledge the role of the individual and that the root cause of destitution was often just a failure of character. It was this fundamental disagreement about the causes of poverty that resulted in the split. Outside the commission, the liberal press and the unions tended to support the minority view while the medical profession and welfare philanthropists with their voluntary aid committees sided with the majority.

What is surprising is that when it came to the Liberal party reforms, most working people where either indifferent or against the idea of state welfare. The trade unions argued that what was needed was decent wages for workers that could facilitate self-help, not hand outs from a state that most felt was run by the rich to serve the needs of the rich. Ministers were suspected of supporting social welfare because it was cheaper than actually providing workers with a good living wage and regular employment.

The mixed experiences of those on state relief seemed to support this view. The poor law was generally loathed as was universal education, which deprived the poor of badly needed income from their children. Housing clearances were also disliked by some for appearing to make more people homeless than they housed.

At the turn of the century, the largest working class organisations were the friendly societies. In 1900, their membership numbered 5.6 million compared to 1.2 million trade union members. Friendly societies provided their members with insurance against ill-health and old age and so clearly they had a vested interest in the idea of state provision of pensions and sickness benefits.

The dominant view was that self-help provided by friendly societies, mutual organisations and trade union provision was morally preferable to relying on an overly intrusive state. In reality the trade unions could be as intrusive as any form of poor relief. Anyone on sick relief and so drawing money out of the union pot would be closely monitored within the community to ensure they were not malingering. A "brother" from the local trade union committee would regularly visit someone on sickness benefit to ensure they were not working on the side or that they were not drinking too much or even if they were going out on a Sunday to anywhere other than a church.

The working classes also questioned who was paying for all these state welfare reforms. Much of the government revenue was coming from indirect taxes on tea, sugar, alcohol and cocoa which were being disproportionately paid by working people. What is interesting is how the distrust of welfare reform felt by the working classes and their institutions in the 1900s had disappeared by the time the welfare state arrived in the 1940s.

The two Royal Commission reports were published on the 2nd February 1909. The majority report seemed to get a more positive press reaction. The Webbs, exhausted, retreated to Italy for six week to recuperate. On their return in May, they set up the National Committee for the Break up of the Poor Law which later became the National Committee for the Prevention of Destitution. Beatrice and Sidney Webb along with their fellow Fabians launched a national lecture tour in support of the minority report along with study circles, correspondence classes and a lending library for supporters. The committee was at its most popular by 1910 with 30,000 signed up members.

But as the Liberal reforms were passed the momentum for poor law abolition waned until the National Committee for the Break up of the Poor Law had its final meeting on 19th September 1912. The Webbs shifted tactics and decided to hitch their star to the Independent Labour Party by setting up a joint committee between it and the Fabians for a "War on Poverty" campaign.

But it was the First World War that in the end overshadowed poor law reform. As surplus labour was absorbed by the war effort so the workhouses emptied and the casual wards closed. The numbers of paupers claiming any type of relief had fallen steadily to 450,000 by 1918.

One hundred years on, as the Liberal/Conservative coalition pulls together its welfare reforms the issues have little changed. With an annual welfare bill of £60bn cost is once more driving reform. Alleged "welfare dependency" is as central to today's debate as it was a hundred years ago. And, because of the existence of 800,000 long-term unemployed, the state is seeking to distinguish between those who can't work and those who don't want to work, between the deserving and the undeserving poor.

The architect of the coalition reforms, Secretary of State for Work and Pensions, Iain Duncan Smith, talks of a new contract between state and the individual in which, in return for assistance, you make a commitment to take work or else sanctions will be imposed. Rowan Williams, Archbishop of Canterbury, concerned about changes to housing benefit and job seekers allowance feels it necessary to remind us that people are in difficult circumstance "not because they are wicked stupid or lazy but because circumstance have been against them". Social attitude surveys that track changing attitudes to welfare have, since the mid-1980s, monitored our steady decline in sympathy towards the unemployed.

The morality of poverty is back and our notion of the deserving and undeserving poor is today as central to the debate as it was to the Edwardians.

*Stuart Spear*

CHAPTER 10

# Port Health

*The diseases to which sailors are peculiarly liable fall under four headings:*
*(a) Those which are caused by the peculiar stresses of the work, the liability to Hernia and Aneurism of Sailors, and "Fireman's Frenzy".*
*(b) Those attending the vices to which sailors in foreign ports are particularly subject, Alcoholism and Venereal Diseases.*
*(c) Tropical Diseases, including Malaria, Beri Beri, Plague and Cholera.*
*(d) Those associated with the peculiar environment of the sailor, such as Rheumatism – the "Sailor's Curse" – due to defective and damp forecastles; Enteric Fever and Dysentery, often... due to the close association of the sick with the healthy in the confined quarters on shipboard; Phthisis [TB] due to deficient lighting and ventilation, and the opportunity for easy infection.*
    *Report of the Port Medical Officer of Health, Liverpool, 1909*

Port health remains one of the most interesting specialisms in all public health work. One hundred years ago, when world trade depended on shipping and with few rules about safety on boats, it was a fascinating, diverse and sometimes dangerous career. This chapter gives some (often grisly) details of the most important tasks at the time, especially those to prevent deadly contagious diseases being brought in from abroad, overseeing conditions in the often chaotic and inebriated life lived around the ports, and trying to preserve the health of sailors and migrants. So, in what kind of world did the port sanitary officers live?

In 1911, Britain's huge empire and prodigious manufacturing capabilities depended on its shipping routes, and British ports formed the hub of a newly expanded global trade. The tonnage of ships visiting British ports had increased sevenfold over the previous half-century to 139 million tons, and nearly half of the total world carrying-capacity at sea was owned by British companies. Maritime technology was changing too: by 1910, well over 90 per cent of ships docking in Britain were steam-powered, and improved design and technology meant that the cost of freight was less than it had ever been before. Transporting wheat and sugar from the colonies, for example, cost less than a farthing a pound (£0.00104). Britain was importing huge amounts of foodstuffs: for example, in 1910, more than four million beef carcasses and 13 million sheep and lamb carcasses (we were far from self-sufficient in food even then). The boats leaving our ports were carrying not only goods for export but hundreds of thousands of desperately poor people, hoping for a better life in the colonies or the USA. In 1909, over 312,000 emigrants left from Liverpool alone. The conditions of shipping were still extremely hazardous and problematic. Many ships were lost each year; many cargoes perished before they could reach port; many seamen lost their lives or their health by drowning, accidents, or as a consequence of the living conditions on the ships. The vastly bigger international trade brought an increased risk of the spread of diseases such as cholera, plague and smallpox to the ports of trading countries, as they were still endemic in many parts of the world.

Trade hub: Newcastle was a busy port in the Edwardian period

To deal with such apparent chaos and risk, by 1911, Britain had developed with its port sanitary authorities the first reliable, preventative health systems for ports that were compatible with the speed of modern trading. They provided a dedicated, targeted and flexible means of protection against disease that was known as the "English system" and was widely admired internationally.

The old method of combating the spread of deadly diseases from other countries had been the system of quarantine, first developed in Venice in the 14th century after the Black Death had devastated the city. Ships arriving from lands where disease was rife would be detained in an isolated place, well away from Venice, for 40 days (quaranta means 40). While the occupants waited, the cargo would be unloaded and treated by airing or fumigating in various ways. After 40 days without sign of disease, ships were granted pratique, the licence to enter port.

This system, or variants of it, was used across Europe through the centuries, although it was never efficient and its critics could always point to examples where it had not worked. A ship would be given a "clean bill" if and when it was free of the disease, and a "foul bill" if not. In some ways quarantining was foolish, for, if there were disease aboard, the people still unaffected would be held in the same area as the affected, and so were at considerable extra risk of contracting the disease. It was also hugely expensive, eating up profits and holding up trade.

During the 19th century, advances in scientific understanding of diseases and public pressure to act, particularly to protect against the spread of typhoid, finally led to Public Health Acts in 1872 and 1875 that created separate port sanitary authorities for each port. The work of each port sanitary authority was led by a port medical officer of health, whose skill and dedication were crucial to what was achieved. Some of them were outstanding figures. Each was supported by port sanitary inspectors and often further staff, such as generalist sanitary inspectors or specialist rat catchers. Quarantine was finally formally replaced by legislation in 1896, with a set of stipulated medical inspection procedures. The port health teams faced immense tasks yet were crippled by the constraints on their expenditure and resources.

Each port sanitary authority was governed by a local board made up of members of the adjoining, inland, sanitary authorities, which had to make financial contributions towards the running of the system. By the end of the 19th century Truro and Falmouth Board, for example, had 16 members: six from Falmouth Borough, one from

Penryn Borough, four from Truro City, one from Falmouth Union Rural Sanitary District, one from Helston Union Rural Sanitary District and three from Truro Union Rural Sanitary District. With so many local notables overseeing payments, it is not likely that they wasted any money.

By 1911, the benefits of the English system seemed patent when compared to the terrible consequences of the less thoroughgoing systems operating in some parts of the world. In South Africa, for example, the consequences of a lapse in vigilance in preventative public health had been terrifying. During the Second Boer War (1899-1902), the ports and railways there were "bursting at the seams with wartime commerce, and with an influx of refugees from the interior and large numbers of migrant labourers". Infected rats from South America entered South African ports, bringing cases of bubonic plague to Cape Town and Port Elizabeth.

The disease then spread along the railway system, reaching as far north as current-day Zimbabwe and Botswana. With every effort going towards the prosecution of the war, there was little spare manpower for the authorities to deal with the epidemic, and with a colonial society highly differentiated along lines of race and class, control measures were based more on racial fears than rational consideration of the methods by which diseases spread. The white population saw segregation as a way of protecting themselves. In fact, it was an unsuccessful measure – people invariably mix – that just reinforced social mistrust and misinformation. Shamefully, in some cases frightened African communities were fobbed off with accounts that the disease was not severe.

Even this epidemic paled in comparison to the horror of northern China in the winter of 1910, when bubonic plague, which was endemic in tarbagans (a kind of marmot, hunted for its fur, and far easier to kill when exhausted with infection) passed, via the fleas on infected pelts, to the human population and spread along the trade routes for fur-dealing, causing more than 50,000 deaths.

In contrast, people felt great security in the system of protection at British ports, for it depended on research, skilled medical staff, reliable teamwork and superb networking with sanitary authorities inland where necessary. Luck was a factor, too, of course, although this was not stressed.

The system worked in this way. The port medical officer of health would collect intelligence of all outbreaks of serious contagious diseases occurring anywhere in the world, and would maintain a list of infected ports, which was used by the river pilots when they boarded incoming ships. They would ask the ship's captain three questions: if the ship had called at any of the infected ports, whether there had been any infectious sickness on board in the previous 28 days (including sick people who had been left along the route), and if there were, was anyone on board still sick? If the answers to these questions were all no, the ship could dock.

If the answer was "yes" to even one question, the ship was immediately required to fly a special signal and use special lights at night, thus warning others they it was "foul" whilst identifying its location for the port medical officer of health, who would board and inspect crew and passengers. He could demand their removal to hospital, compulsory vaccinations, destruction of rodents, burning of contaminated bedding, cleaning of drinking-water tanks, and the disinfection or fumigation of parts or all of the vessel. Only then would the ship be permitted to dock. When it did dock, all those uninfected were free to go, although careful record was made of their intended destinations.

Many port sanitary authorities would have their own hospitals for those infected. This was sometimes a "floating hospital", often a barge with a tiny ward for the sick and a full-time nurse. Some, for example in London or Liverpool, were substantial and gained an international reputation for their standards of treatment. Many patients, of course, never left these hospitals alive: in Falmouth and Truro, the original port hospital was handily situated next to a local cemetery.

In fact, the squabble about who should pay for this medical care led to a major public health development. The costs were met by the nearby local authorities, and being parsimonious, they wanted central government to pay. Organising the lobbying for this led to the creation of the Association of Port Sanitary Authorities which still exists and is known today as the Association of Port Health Authorities. (Eventually the local authorities won back half the costs of the hospitals.)

The efficiency of the English system is demonstrated by the way in which it prevented the spread of what was probably the last active case of plague in a British port. In September, 1912, the SS Bellailsa docked in Hamburg from Rosario, having visited Monte Video, St. Vincent and Tenerife en route. There were four young apprentices on board, three sleeping in adjacent berths, the fourth separately on the other side of the ship. The three had bought a pet rabbit in Rosario and used to play with it in their bunks. While in Hamburg, the animal died and was thrown overboard. Later, one of the boys, Robert Morton, became very ill, Although a doctor attended, he died and his body was taken ashore.

Four days later, out at sea, the second of the three, John McWhirter, became so ill, the captain put him ashore at Cuxhaven, at the mouth of the Elbe, where he, too, died. The boat arrived in Newcastle-upon-Tyne on 10th September, and shortly after, the third of the rabbit-owners, John Raeburn, fell ill. At this stage, no one understood why. The port medical officer, Edmund Harker, gave a preliminary diagnosis of enteric fever, but as a precaution ordered the patient removed to the floating hospital and the fumigation of all the crew spaces and cleaning of water tanks. Everyone else on board appeared healthy and was allowed to leave for their various homes across the UK, having left details of their destinations.

John Raeburn's condition worsened and Dr Harker, noting enlargement of a deep lymphatic gland in his throat, began to suspect plague, although blood tests were inconclusive. Within days, the boy developed double pneumonia. The College of Medicine in Newcastle, having been alerted to the case, inoculated a guinea pig with cultures from his blood – the animal died within 48 hours and examination revealed plague bacteria. The boy died and an immediate post-mortem and prompt burial followed, strict precautions being taken throughout. Two days after the funeral, a letter was received from the port doctor of Hamburg: re-examination of samples from the other two boys had revealed bubonic plague. The port sanitary officers were therefore given the considerable task of contacting medical officers of health across the country and organising careful surveillance of the dock area itself. Fortunately, no more cases were found. The ship was carefully re-fumigated and 12 rats collected and tested. Only one, found in the area directly under the berths of the three boys, was infected with plague. The fourth apprentice, who slept on the opposite side of the boat, was unaffected.

Dr Harker surmised that rats aboard would have had access to the rabbit and been attracted by its ready food supply and that the rabbit was infected with plague, possibly before arriving on board ship. It was later learnt that in Hamburg, a workman had offered to buy the rabbit from the apprentices for his own children, but it had died in the night before he could collect it.

Whilst protection against importation of dangerous diseases was the flagship task of the port sanitary inspectors, their other tasks, especially given their small numbers and status, were also enormous in scope, and very challenging, if not grim.

It must be remembered that the people whom we now think of as the predecessors of the present members of the Chartered Institute of Environmental Health, were only a part, and a fairly lowly part, of the port sanitary system, which operated under strict rules of law, and, in Edwardian times, etiquette. They observed and they reported, but it was always the medical officers who held the power, as this letter from "An Old Inspector" in The Sanitary Journal from 1909 makes clear: "If I understand the order of the Local Government Board, every Sanitary Inspector is... the absolute servant of the Medical Officer, and as such he stands in readiness to obey... The only thing he can do is to keep his eyes and ears open and if he, by so doing, hears of a case that has not come to the knowledge of the Medical Officer of Health, he can quietly put it before his notice, and then await his orders." This must have been frustrating, for all port sanitary inspectors had experience at sea and most also had public-health qualifications. Several colleges ran "Courses of Instruction in Sanitary Science", examined by MoHs, surveyors and engineers.

Like most aspects of public health, however, the work was far from glamorous and perhaps its status rubbed off on the men. There were serious problems with the public health provision for those living around the ports, often in rundown, damp and filthy barges in small inlets. Whole families might live in tiny cabins, with little light or ventilation and what The Lancet described as "not even the ghost of a sanitary regulation". In 1909, Liverpool allocated one inspector one day a week to deal solely with canal boats, inspecting 769 of them.

In 1908, came a major change to port health work. For the first time, the port sanitary inspectors had, with customs officers, duties to inspect food imports. The amounts in differing ports were huge. The inventory for 1908 lists, in value, over £2.6 million of live animals, £5 million of bacon (at Liverpool), £2.6 million of fresh beef imported at Southampton, and £62,000 of poultry and game at Hull.

Meticulous records were kept of food examined, regarded as suspicious and released, or destroyed; it is interesting that alternative purposes were found for much food that today might simply be thrown away. For example, in Weymouth in 1920, 30 boxes of oats were released "for industrial purposes only", two quarters of cheese were released "for trimming", 36 lbs of margarine were released for soap-making and 1,145 lbs of wheat went for animal food.

The port sanitary inspectors would also inspect the live animals that arrived in port. William Hanna, in his Report on Marine Hygiene, wrote in 1917: "During the winter and spring months, much serious and unnecessary injury is inflicted on animals during transit by boat from Ireland to England. Animals are thrown about during rough weather and many of them are suffocated. This more frequently occurs with sheep; and broken limbs are often reported, especially among pigs." The landing of live cattle took up the whole time of one inspector at Liverpool in 1909: he supervised 148,233 live cattle and more than 8,000 sheep landings, and equivalent numbers slaughtered at the "Foreign Animals Wharf". One can only imagine the conditions on the swaying boats where the terrified animals were packed together.

Ships were routinely infested with rats, and given their importance as potential carriers of the plague bacterium carrying fleas, their destruction was a top priority. Rat catchers were deployed in the docks and measures taken included rat guards on hawsers and painting gangplanks white. Fumigation of ships was often done with cyanide, a very hazardous procedure that had to be done according to strict procedures and with great care. The practice was regarded as routine and even used for verminous houses; in 1935, two little girls died when their home was fumigated but their bedding not adequately aired before they went to bed.

Enforcing sanitary conditions for those on board ship was another of the enormous tasks given to the port sanitary inspectors. Hundreds of thousands of Britons were leaving for "British North America", Australia, New Zealand, India or other British colonies and possessions. In 1905, from Liverpool alone, 99,930 people left for other parts of the British Empire, 90 per cent of them to Canada. They were classified as 66,344 English, 2,689 Scotch, 1,101 Irish, 24,886 "Foreigners" and 4,910 "Not distinguished". One wonders what "not distinguished" meant.

There were also arriving in British ports tens of thousands of migrants escaping poverty in Eastern Europe intending to stay in Britain or, more generally, "transmigrants" en route for the USA, South Africa or Argentina, and subject to strict rules that they must not settle in the UK. (The ship owner was legally responsible for ensuring this.) The scale of these movements of people was astounding: between 1880 and 1914 it was estimated that one million Jewish transmigrants alone arrived at easterly British ports, and crossed the country to take steamships from ports such as Glasgow, Liverpool, Southampton and London. The tickets were cheap – crossing to New York might cost as little as £2 10s per person – and conditions were overcrowded and squalid.

All emigrants travelling second class or steerage would be inspected by medical officers from the Board of Trade, accompanied by a port sanitary inspector, who would supervise the removal to hospital of anyone rejected because of actual or suspected disease. They suffered from conditions including chickenpox, whooping cough, diphtheria, trachoma, psychosis, scabies and "lunacy", and their families would have had to make hard decisions as to what to do.

A major, almost insuperable task for the port sanitary inspectors concerned the conditions for seamen. In 1912, there were more than 209,000 seafarers on British ships alone and the state of the ships was often parlous, with the port MoH for Newport, Monmouthshire, reporting one in six vessels as being insanitary. Two years later, the MoH for the Port of London compared the conditions for seamen on many vessels to those of cave dwellers in prehistoric times. To quote the academic Dr Sally Sheard, they experienced "damp, filthy and overcrowded cabins, lack of ventilation, deficient heating… inadequate diets, lack of on-board medical care and poor safety standards".

The crew of an ordinary cargo steamer in 1912 would typically be about 77, with 43 working on deck. The remainder worked in the engine room, covered in a mixture of sweat and coal-dust, shovelling coal into the boilers, and shovelling ash out, entirely by hand. It has been estimated that each fireman would shovel around two tons of coal in every four-hour watch, working two watches a day. The conditions in which men slept and ate were very cramped, with around 16 inches allowed for the width of a hammock. If emigrants were on board, there would be around 40 extra crew and stewards, thus making conditions below deck even more constricted. Facilities for cooking were rudimentary and rarely hygienic, facilities for washing often entirely absent. Contrast this with the luxurious fare for first-class passengers on liners, who would have early morning tea or coffee, breakfast, "tiffin" at 12 o'clock, afternoon tea and seven-course dinners.

Despite the furore over the Titanic disaster in 1912 and the measures introduced by the first International Safety Conference a year afterwards (that each ocean-going passenger vessel must have a radio and sufficient lifeboats for all), in 1913, it was estimated that a seaman was 20 times more likely than a passenger to die from shipwreck and 25 times more likely to die from an accident.

Conditions were so bad that an increasing proportion of crews came from abroad, a cause of concern in the press who called for "British seamen for British ships" (but did not necessarily make the link to appalling working conditions and low pay as a reason). Whilst around a sixth of seamen did come from other foreign countries, a quarter were sailors originating from India or South Asia and known as "lascars". There was a long history of lascars serving on British ships and they were so much a part of the fabric of port life that they were not generally classified as foreigners. They had been coming to Britain in their thousands ever since the 17th century, many settling here and marrying British women, so that there were established communities in many ports.

By 1914, there were 51,616 lascars in Britain. They were subject to particularly harsh terms of service, with special lascar agreements on British ships allowing ship-owners to retain a man in service for up to three years at a time and to transfer him between ships at will.

Legislation had increased the powers of port sanitary inspectors. By 1911, they could inspect all the vessels in port "to examine into their sanitary state and the health of those on board", and this included checking on food supplies and all seamen's lodging houses. But there were tiny numbers of inspectors compared to the vast numbers of ships visiting the ports. Boats stayed only a short time in port and despite prodigious number of inspections – in 1909, 4,010 vessels were visited in Liverpool, on which were found 1,938 serious defects of construction, repair or dirt – rigorous enforcement was impossible. Even in the 1920s, inspectors from the Board of Trade were still recording that crews on board British ships would be unlikely to find hot water, heating or even drying space for wet clothes. Water for the crew might still be held in tanks accessed from the deck surface, so that when they were filled, dirt from the decks got inside. Flushing lavatories were a rarity, clean ones almost non-existent.

The campaign for improvements in the seamen's lot was a long and bitter one, so much so that sailors were central to historically important industrial unrest across the UK. Havelock Wilson formed their first union in 1887 – men could be sacked for belonging – but little progress was made. The ship-owners were intransigent. In the early 20th century, however, several factors changed. There was increased membership and militancy of trade unions generally. In 1904, Wilson's union reformed as the National Sailors' and Firemen's Union, and, crucially, affiliated to the strong International Transport Workers' Federation, the TWF, organised by Tom Mann and Benn Tillet. In 1906, the Trade Disputes Act removed many legal impediments from unions; in particular, the right to strike was strengthened. The stage was set for disputes.

A particularly resented aspect of the seamen's lot in which the port sanitary authorities were involved was the degrading way in which the men were required to undergo medical inspections. The inspections were, for many, the last straw. At the end of May, 1911, the National Sailors and Firemen's Union and the National Union of Ships' Stewards, Cooks, Butchers and Bakers (both affiliated to the TWF) went on strike in Liverpool, initially only because of the degrading medical inspections, but later adding demands for improved living accommodation, union recognition and better wages.

On 14th June, the crews of two US liners docked in Liverpool refused to sign on for work; their action was copied almost immediately by crews in Southampton. The same day, Tom Mann, leader of the International Transport Workers' Federation, addressed a famous meeting of the first set of strikers with the cry, "War declared! Strike for Liberty!" Within 24 hours, seamen at most major British ports and even some abroad, including in Belgium and Holland, were out. A general transport strike began, paralysing commerce.

Within weeks, the shipping companies signalled agreement to the strikers' demands. Inspired, the dockers, too, struck for improved pay and conditions, and seamen went back on strike to support them! The employers' Shipping Federation capitulated, with general agreement to improved rates of pay, reduced working hours and an end to discrimination against union members (the right to sack them merely for belonging was removed). Industrial unrest, some of it widespread, continued through the summer of 1911, with more major strikes across transport industries in August.

Yet the medical examinations have to be explained. Whilst the rates of illness and accident were extraordinarily high, these were not the problems of seamen's health given most priority. Over the early years of the 20th century there were significant improvements in the diagnosis and treatment of venereal diseases. This nled to public health drives to improve provision for sufferers and introduce preventative measures. The subject held fear, horror and fascination. It was commonly believed that seamen were particularly liable to have such diseases (we have no way of knowing whether this was true), hence their routine and humiliating compulsory examination upon arriving in port.

The extent of embedded ignorance, shame and irrationality about venereal diseases was staggering: it was widely believed, for example, that a man could be cured by having intercourse with a virgin. The report of the Royal Commission on Venereal Disease in 1916 estimating that a tenth of the British urban population was infected with syphilis and even more with gonorrhoea. After this, local authorities began to open free clinics and quack treatments were outlawed. For sailors, however, given their constant travelling, this was of little use. Thomas Howard, the port MoH for Weymouth, wrote in 1920: "One of the difficulties... is that many of the ships are only in port for a few days, and it often happens that the clinic is not available when the men apply for treatment. This is very unfortunate in the case of a man with a primary chancre who may be away from his home port for two or three months and is ignorant of the consequences resulting from neglect of early treatment. At present, I see no practical solution to this difficulty."

Other health problems endured by men at sea improved only slowly. Sally Sheard has argued that "the statistically more serious [health problems], most of which resulted from their working and living conditions on vessels, did not receive the same degree of attention, precisely because they had no wider public health implications."

It was to take a further 20 years and major strikes before legislation was introduced that improved general standards – most shipowners had no interest in measures that merely added to their costs without bringing a return.

These can only be snapshots of the enormously varied work done by the port sanitary inspectors a century ago. Their services extended, adding the new "ports" of the air services. But port health officers continue to inspect vessels to ensure hygienic conditions on board and to check for infectious diseases on incoming planes and ships. They still have tiny numbers compared to the magnitude of these tasks, and the risk of pandemics has not disappeared. There are around 110 million arrivals at our airports each year in Britain from other countries and more than a quarter of a million people arrive from places where there is a high risk of tuberculosis.

Consider that at Gatwick alone, in a typical year, there are more than 35 million passenger movements and 270,000 aircraft movements, involving 90 airlines and 200 destinations. The major tasks of the port health inspectors also include inspecting imported food, and all food manufacturing and catering in ports and airports. They also license nearby shellfish beds and continue to deal with statutory nuisances within each port area. We have many reasons to be grateful for their diligence, for the excellent systems of cooperation between port health authorities and for their efficiency in dealing with these enormous tasks.

*Ava Greenwell*

# AFTERWORD

*There's no greater sign of insanity than to simply carry on doing the same thing over and over and to expect a different result.*

*Albert Einstein*

I was grateful for the chance to write this afterword – the study of history has been a passion of mine for even longer than environmental health. Apart from the insights into politics and the rise and fall of civilisations it provides, there is the history of how people lived their lives and what it would have been like to be born over 100 years ago. As all my grandparents were adults during the Edwardian period, there are family memories passed on directly that told me what it was like to be living then.

History is important – as George Santayana said in 1905: "Those who cannot remember the past are condemned to repeat it." There are three things that have made the human race the world's dominant species: the fact that we are social animals who can work as a group and share tasks; our opposable thumbs that enable us to make clothes and tools to tame unfriendly environments; and, most importantly, our ability to use symbols and to share information and pass it on down the generations. All of those three key strengths are relevant to understanding and dealing with the threats to public health, both new and old.

I joined local government in 1974, a year that many hoped would usher in a brave new world for environmental health. At a time when local government was structured around professional departments, this was our chance to join the club! The pre-1974 structure was one that our Edwardian colleagues would have substantially recognised – as was some of the legislation then deployed (the Public Health Act 1936 largely served to reconsolidate that from 1875). One of the most powerful books I read as a student EHO was Cruel Habitations by Enid Gauldie, a study of working class housing between 1780 and 1918. This set out very clearly what it was like for the majority of the population. While we often focus on the slums of the inner cities, the conditions of the rural poor were more likely to be overlooked, but often as bad.

In my early days as a student and as a district EHO, it was common to come across elderly people who still remembered the operation of the poor law. This was one of the things that stopped them claiming benefits or other entitlements – or anything that smacked of "going on the parish". Even after the poor law had long gone, it continued to sting like a dead wasp – it can be argued that the planning of council estates to replace the cleared slums was for a long time affected by similar attitudes: the idea that such communities should participate in developing these schemes was a long time coming.

Some of the social arguments spread across our tabloids would also resonate with our Edwardian predecessors – drawing a distinction between the "deserving" and the "undeserving" poor was a feature then as now. Indeed with Places for People (a large social housing provider) having recently raised capital for new dwellings by issuing bonds that offer a return to investors, we are right back to the start of the Housing Association movement and Octavia Hill.

We should never forget poverty. It can be argued that Edwin Chadwick's fixation with connections between miasma, dirt and public health clouded this issue. W.P. Alison's paper of 1842, Observations on the Generation of Fever, and Neil Arnott's evidence to the Select Committee on the Health of Towns, both underlined that poverty was actually at the root of housing problems in the 19th century.

In essence, there will always be a part of society that cannot afford to house itself decently or possibly at all. There are only four policy options and all four have been tried. More than once. We subsidise rents, we subsidise buildings, we let standards drop to what is affordable, or we let homelessness increase. Or a mixture of these. It is difficult to look enthusiastic when a new minister or civil servant brightly claims to have come up with a new approach that is actually no such thing. From the perspective of environmental health, reducing standards or increasing overcrowding or homelessness are no options at all.

The Edwardian period was a period of change, and was also the interregnum between the Victorian age and the First World War. The reforming parliament under the Liberals introduced unemployment benefits and old age pensions as well as attacking the balance of power between the Commons and the Lords – the era had started with a Marquess as Prime Minister.

So what's changed? With the Marmot Review of 2010 already

apparently gathering dust and cuts to public spending likely to impact on the needier parts of the population disproportionately, we still have clear inequalities of wealth and health. The last few years have widened the gap between the rich and the "squeezed middle", and, as Marmot showed, inequalities of health spread across the social gradient. One of my fears for the future is linked to the growth of antibiotic resistant strains of bacteria, which have reached such proportions that they can be found even in Antarctica. For those in the west, the old bacterial scourges of the Edwardian period and before have largely disappeared. This brief time of protection may prove to have been the interlude in a long battle. In other parts of the world, these threats have never gone away. It could be argued that we have largely thrown this boon away by the way we have used these drugs. Climate change could affect our lives in all sorts of ways including reintroducing some old foes to the UK, such as malaria, as well as some new ones. Again, other parts of the world have never known such freedoms.

Looking to the future, we are again going through a period of change in which many structures and certainties are being tested. As a profession, environmental health has come a long way but some of its old enemies are still recognisable. New ones have come along. In some of my talks, I use slides of London air quality, comparing Trafalgar Square during the smog of the 1950s to a picture from this decade in which the sun is shining – and yet the threat of the new invisible pollutants is worse than that from the old in terms of the excess deaths.

The Edwardian equivalents to today's environmental health practitioners were very much creatures of local government. Over the last 25 years, the proportion of members of the Chartered Institute of Environmental Health working for businesses, or providing support and training to the private sector has steadily grown. The concept of earned recognition has gained traction as a further method of focusing regulators on the worst and riskiest businesses. Whatever we may think about the past, methods of delivering environmental health will become more varied and we need to adapt ourselves to stay relevant in a changing world. With public health returning to local government – and whatever happens to the Health and Social Care Bill and to health secretary, Andrew Lansley, this part of the proposals is likely to go forward one way or the other – there is a great opportunity for environmental health practitioners to reclaim their public health heritage.

I want environmental health to survive as a discrete body of knowledge and as a profession, and I believe that our skills are still hugely relevant to tackling the issues of our times. Our success depends on how well we take forward the battles of our predecessors and how we refocus on the outcomes we want to achieve. Each of the three human key skills I referred to at the beginning plays a part in this, and, for me, sharing information and evidence, as well as experiences of successes and failures, plays a big part in that. This timely and vivid publication, The Stuff of Life, helps to remind us how we became what we are now.

*Tim Everett,*
*Chartered Environmental Health Practitioner*

# CHRONOLOGY

*Note: The Victorian period is included because it provided the social and legislative foundations for Edwardian public health improvement.*

**1848** Public Health Act creates a national General Board of Health (abolished in 1853) and requires the appointment of inspectors of nuisances by local boards of health.

**1871** Creation of the Local Government Board. Takes over responsibilities for local government and those of the previous Poor Law Board.

**1872** Public Health Act. Defines sanitary authorities as either town councils or Poor Law Boards of Guardians.

**1875** Artisans and Labourers Dwellings Improvement or Cross Act (and 1879) gives authorities powers to clear and reconstruct unhealthy areas, using compulsory purchase powers. Follows the Liberals' Torrens Act of 1868.

Disraeli's Public Health Act. Codifies previous regulations on sewage, drainage, public lavatories and cellar dwellings. Section 157 covers by-laws, which are now to be created by the Local Government Board, which issues model by-laws in 1877. Compulsory medical officers of health in every sanitary authority in England and Wales.

**1876** Rivers Pollution Act prohibits the disposal of solid matter, liquid or solid sewage, or drainage from mines and factories into streams if injurious to health.

**1878** Factory and Workshops Act. No labour and education for children under 10. Restrictions on female labour.

**1883** Edwin Chadwick made president of the Association of Public Sanitary Inspectors. He urges members to collect local information and to lobby their MPs.

**1884** Third Reform Act. Working men in the country, including labourers given parliamentary vote. Adds 2.6 million voters to the electorate, taking the total to almost six million.

Royal Society for the Prevention of Cruelty to Children formed.

The Royal Commission on the Housing of the Working Classes details the appalling living conditions of the Victorian poor, including "house farming".

**1887 } 1897 }** Victoria's golden and diamond jubilees.

**1888** Local Government Act. Sixty-two county councils formed, directly elected by ratepayers, with a universal male franchise. Urban reforms of 1835 thus extended to countryside.

London County Council set up. Becomes socially reforming body, dominated by Progressives from 1889 to 1907 when Moderates take over.

The Life and Labour of the People of London, by Charles Booth. Appears in 17 volumes up until 1903.

**1890** Housing of the Working Classes Act. Passed at the instigation of the new London County Council. Stronger house clearance, unfitness and rebuilding powers. Part three allows councils to build new lodging houses (which can be separate houses or cottages). London's authorities are now the LCC and the City of London Commissioners of Sewers. No exchequer subsidy until 1919.

Chadwick receives a birthday dinner from the association, is awarded a knighthood and dies. His son, Osbert, carries out sanitary work in India.

**1891** Education Act. School fees for elementary schools abolished. Mainly the work of Joseph Chamberlain.

**1892** European cholera epidemic leaves London unscathed. Shows efficacy of sanitary reforms.

**1893** Appointment of women sanitary inspectors in London boroughs and of the first lady factory inspectors.

**1894** Counties are divided into urban and rural districts converted from former sanitary authorities. Parishes set up as third-tier authorities. Women can serve on parish and urban district councils and women ratepayers can vote.

Cilfynydd mine disaster in South Wales – 260 people killed.

**1896** Women Sanitary Inspectors' Association founded on an informal basis.

**1899** Employers' Liability Act.

Seebohm Rowntree's research into poverty in York.

London Government Act. Metropolitan borough councils replace parish vestries and district boards of works, taking over their chief medical officers. Only 11 of the 28 new borough councils build housing by 1913.

**1900** Housing of the Working Classes Act. Amends 1890 legislation. London powers extended to provincial boroughs. Councils can build outside their districts.

**1901** 22 January. Death of Queen Victoria.

Factory and Workshop Act. Minimum working age up to 12.

Taff Vale judgement. House of Lords awards £23,000 against the Amalgamated Society of Railway Servants.

**1902** Smallpox outbreak in London kills more than 2,000.
Vaccination programme launched.

June. Coronation of Edward VII.

Balfour's Education Act transfers all school boards' powers
to county and borough councils, which set up education
committees. In London, the LCC merges with the London
School Board.

Midwives Act.

**1903** Women's Social and Political Union set up by Emmeline
Pankhurst. Calls for votes for women. Becomes the
suffragette movement in 1906.

**1904** Royal Commission on the Care and Control of the Feeble-
minded. (Reports in 1908). Lobbying from county and
borough councils and education committees to pass a bill
to restrict the breeding of the "unfit". Eugenics Education
Society begins.

Women's Sanitary Inspectors' Association formally
constituted.

**1905** Royal Commission on the Poor Laws and the Relief of
Distress.

Unemployed Workmen's Act. Allows local authorities to help
the unemployed with money from the rates.

**1906** February. Election victory for Liberals under Sir Henry
Campbell Bannerman. The Labour Representation
Committee, led by Keir Hardy, which soon becomes the
Labour party, wins 29 seats, including John Burns, London
County Council councillor.

Free school meals in elementary schools – not compulsory.

Women's Sanitary Inspectors' Association membership extended to provinces.

**1907** Notification of Births Act (becomes compulsory in 1915).

**1908** Suffragettes raid ministers' houses, petition the king and chain themselves to railings. Largest ever suffragette demonstration – 200,000 women in Hyde Park.

Old age pensions.

Royal Sanitary Institute institutes examinations in health-visiting.

**1909** People's Budget raises taxes and introduces a land tax. Rejected by the House of Lords.

Housing and Town Planning Act. Gives councils town-planning powers for new developments. Stronger powers for sanitary inspectors. Five per cent companies have access to low-interest loans.

Report of the Royal Commission on the Poor Laws reveals high mortality rates in workhouses. Majority report wishes to retain the poor law but to devolve its functions. Minority report urges abolition of the poor law and a free health service. The poor law survives until 1929.

Labour Exchanges opened by new Home Secretary Winston Churchill.

**1910** January. People's Budget blocked by the Lords. Crisis.

April. Budget passed. Edward VII dies eight days later.

May. Death of Edward VII.

December. Second general election. Liberals tie with

Conservatives. Irish Nationalists and Labour hold balance.

**1911** June. Coronation of George V.

National Insurance Act. Winston Churchill's unemployment scheme, paid for by worker, employer and state. Covers one-in-six of the workforce, mainly in iron, steel and ship-building. Lloyd George's state-backed health insurance, known as "ninepence for fourpence". Covers all male workers between 16 and 70 on less than £160 a year.

MPs are paid salaries.

**1912** Port of London and Medway dockworkers' strike, joined by other transport workers.

**1913** Prisoners Temporary Release Act, the "Cat and Mouse Act", enables hunger-striking women to be released when very ill and returned to prison when they return to health.

**1914** First World War.

**1915** Wartime rent control. Christabel Pankhurst leads a demonstration of 30,000 women in Whitehall to demand the "right to serve".

**1918** Women aged 28 or older with property are given the vote in general elections.

**1919** Ministry of Health begins.

Housing and Town Planning Act (known as Addison Act). Recognises principle of state and ratepayer funding for council housing. The need for 500,000 houses is recognised.

# APPENDIX ONE

## Battle over how to dispose of bodies

*A hundred years ago, burial versus cremation was a hot topic of debate. Few people were cremated, but that was to change thanks to the efforts of determined campaigners.*

A fascinating, if somewhat gruesome article in The Sanitary Journal of April, 1910, is entitled The Sanitary Advantages of Cremation. It was written by T. J. Crofts, a district sanitary inspector in Bristol. Cremation was still an uncommon and somewhat controversial practice in 1910 but Mr Crofts strongly advocates it.

He writes: "No dead body is ever buried within the earth without polluting the soil, the water and the air around and above it." He argues that contagious diseases, such as scarlet fever, typhoid, smallpox, diphtheria and malignant cholera, are transmissible by bacterial means from the buried body: "[Hurtful emanations] have been detected rising to the surface through as much as ten feet of earth."

He notes that: "The air of graveyards has occasionally produced disease; it has been found that in the neighbourhood of our thickly-crowded graveyards the sick rate and death rate have been increased." And he concludes: "I venture to think that few persons can doubt that cremation as a mode of safely decomposing the body after death is at all event the most rapid and efficient agent known."

In 1910, burial was still vastly more popular than cremation. Mr Crofts notes that there are only 13 crematoria in the country. Those in the City of London, Bradford, Hull, Leicester and Sheffield are council-run facilities (Hull opened the first municipal crematorium), while those at Woking, Golder's Green, Glasgow, Manchester, Liverpool, Darlington, Birmingham and Leeds are run by private companies or societies.

A demand for cremation had arisen in Victorian times, due to the gross overcrowding of cities and churchyards. There was strong religious opposition, particularly from the Christian Church, on the grounds that cremation was a pagan practice. This has persisted. The

Roman Catholic Church only lifted its ban on cremation in 1963, and Muslims, Orthodox Jews, and the Greek and Russian Orthodox churches still oppose it.

Those in favour argued their cause with evangelistic zeal and, in 1874, a Cremation Society was set up. It bought some land and built the UK's first crematorium in Woking in Surrey. Professor Gorini of Lodi, Italy, was invited to supervise the erection of the apparatus, assisted by William Eassie, the Cremation Society's Honorary Secretary. The device was successfully tested on the body of a dead horse.

Unfortunately, local people objected and the Home Secretary, Sir Richard Cross, banned the use of the facility, swayed by the argument that cremation could be used to destroy the evidence of a murder victim.

It is here that physician and eccentric Dr William Price of Glamorgan enters the story. Dr Price was a druid, free-love advocate and fanatical vegetarian. Aged 83, he fathered a son by his housekeeper. But the boy, who was called Jesus Christ, died in infancy. On 18th January, 1884, the doctor conducted an outdoor cremation on a hillside overlooking Llantrisant. He performed the rites dressed in white druid's robes over green trousers.

He was arrested and tried, but acquitted. The judge ruled that cremation was legal, providing no nuisance was caused. Dr Price argued in court: "It is not right that a carcass should be allowed to rot and decompose... It results in a wastage of good land, pollution of the earth, water and air, and is a constant danger to all living creatures."

Following the case, the Woking crematorium was used for the first time in 1885 for one Jeannette Pickersgill. In 1902, an Act of Parliament put cremation on an official, legal footing, regulating the practice. However, it remained an unpopular option. Even in 1930, when new Cremation Regulations, which are still in force, were issued fewer than 4 per cent of UK funerals ended in cremation. By 2007, however, the figure had risen to 72 per cent.

*First published in Environmental Health News*
*on 23rd April, 2010, page 36*

## APPENDIX TWO

# Reigate pioneer's battle against scarlet fever

*Infectious diseases were of great concern to the Edwardian sanitary inspector of 1910. Infectious agents were well understood but many died prematurely, especially the young.*

In 1900, more than half of all deaths occurred under the age of 45. In 2009, this had reduced to only 4.4 per cent. The reasons are obvious. Millions of people lived in dirty, overcrowded conditions; mass vaccination had not yet begun; there were no antibiotics; doctors must be paid for; and health visiting was in its infancy.

They may have had the "ologies" – virology, epidemiology, micro-biology – but, in 1910, compulsory disease notification, designed to detect outbreaks and epidemics early and nip them in the bud, was new. Some towns and cities had begun local systems in the 1870s, but national adoptive legislation was not passed until 1889. Notification became compulsory for London in 1891, and the rest of England and Wales in 1899.

The 1889 legislation listed the diseases to be notified as smallpox, cholera, diphtheria, membranous croup, erysipelas, scarlatina or scarlet fever, typhus, typhoid, and enteric, relapsing, continued or puerperal fevers. Certificates were prescribed by the Local Government Board. Local authorities could extend the definition of diseases to be notified and the activities and movements of people with "dangerous infectious disorders" could be restricted. The legislation did not apply to port health authorities.

Originally, heads of household, landlords and doctors had the responsibility to report suspected cases of disease to a "proper officer" in their local authority, normally the medical officer of health. National statistics were collected by the office of the registrar general, which had held data on births, marriages and deaths since 1837.

In the June 1910 Sanitary Journal, Reigate's medical officer of health, Dr A. E. Porter, reflects interestingly on what he sees as the shortcomings of the Infectious Disease (Notification) Act 1889. He also describes in detail a local, scientifically-based programme conducted by sanitary inspectors that is designed to reduced childhood illness.

Dr Porter notes that infant mortality rates have not declined as sharply as general mortality rates since the great 19th century public health acts (1848 and 1875). He observes: "Improvements in sanitary conditions have been accompanied by the virtual disappearance of typhus and relapsing fevers and to a diminution in phthisis and enteric fever... but although the number of deaths from scarlet fever has diminished enormously, probably by 75 per cent, there is no indication that the number of cases has correspondingly decreased."

In addition, he asserts that deaths from diphtheria appear to have increased since compulsory notification. He argues that the Notification Act is failing because it is not picking up cases of the childhood killers early enough.

He calls for schools attendance officers to report absences from school to the local authority, so that sanitary inspectors can carry out home visits and look out for vomiting, sore throats, rashes and swollen glands. "If a doctor is in attendance, it is perhaps a wise policy not to ask for too many details," he adds, tactfully – alluding to the traditional enmity between medical officers and their lesser-paid colleagues, sanitary inspectors.

Through an experiment in Reigate along these lines, Dr Porter has calculated the percentage of cases of diphtheria and scarlet fever missed by notification. He believes that some potentially fatal cases may have been picked up but cannot speak optimistically of other childhood diseases. Measles and whooping cough are infectious before the child shows symptoms, mumps can be mistaken for earache or toothache, and chicken pox can only be detected if each child is stripped to the waist daily.

Cautiously, he concludes of the Reigate experiment: "If anyone is inclined to prophesy that epidemics of scarlet fever and diphtheria will be stamped out by this means, I am afraid he will be proved to be a false prophet, and the failure of the school absentee system will be placed alongside the so-called failure of the Isolation Hospital and the failure of the Notification Act."

*First published in Environmental Health News*
*on 4th June, 2010, page 36*

## APPENDIX THREE

# The case of the unsound carcass

*Does mens rea, or being of guilty mind, apply in food prosecutions?*
*A case heard in 1910 and reported in The Sanitary Journal helped*
*to define its meaning.*

**M**r Hobbs, an army meat contractor, supplied a carcass to a rifle depot in Winchester. It was not a very good carcass – that of a 12-year-old cow with a removed udder. The meat raised suspicions. A sanitary inspector was called in and, following an examination, the carcass was condemned and destroyed.

Proceedings were subsequently taken by the council under Sections 116 and 117 of the Public Health Act (1875), which prohibited the sale of food unfit for human consumption. However, in a magistrates court, the case against Mr Hobbs was dismissed by a majority the bench.

Mr Hobbs now brought a claim for damages against the council under Section 308 of the Public Health Act, arguing that he had lost contracts with the army for the Salisbury Plain barracks, as a result of the condemnation.

The matter was heard by a barrister, acting as an umpire. Finding that "part of the carcass was good and part bad", he upheld Mr Hobbs' claim. In the Divisional Court, Mr Justice Channell ruled that Mr Hobbs was entitled to £800 in damages, with £118 in costs to be paid to him by the council.

Mr Justice Channell upheld the magistrates' dismissal of the case against Mr Hobbs. Only a small part of the carcass, the size of a sixpence, he said, had been diseased. This would have been undetectable by Mr Hobbs and his staff.

For this reason, he could not be held to be in mens rea – that is, of guilty mind – normally a requirement of guilt for imprisonable offences, such as those under Sections 116 and 117 of the Public Health Act.

In what was to become a test case, Hobbs vs the Mayor and Corporation of Winchester, Winchester appealed against the awarding of damages to Mr Hobbs awarded under Section 308. In the Court of Appeal, the council's barrister, Mr Simon, argued that Section 308 was not intended for these kind of proceedings – but, for example, cases where a local authority officer had damaged land through trespass in the process of dealing with a nuisance.

He added that the prosecution for selling unfit meat could have been brought under the Public Health Act by military authorities, in which case, there would have been no recourse for damages against the council.

He asserted: "The umpire had decided that a portion of the meat was unsound; it is monstrous that the butcher should be entitled to come forward to say that the corporation is liable to pay him £800 for seizing that very meat."

Mr Hobbs' barrister, Mr Avery, argued that his client, as maintained by Mr Justice Channel, had not been in default of the Public Health Act, because he had had no knowledge that a portion of the meat sold to the army was unsound. Therefore, he was entitled to damages against the body that had seized and condemned the meat, causing him loss of trade.

Three Appeal Court judges, the Master of the Rolls Lord Justice Farwell and Lord Justice Kennedy unanimously upheld Winchester's appeal. The Master of the Rolls said that Mr Justice Channell had been incorrect in applying the concept of mens rea to cases of selling unfit meat: "Unsound meat was exposed for sale and it was irrelevant to say 'I was not aware of it, or my man did not know it'." Lord Justice Kennedy agreed. He argued that the clear object of The Public Health Act (1875) was to protect buyers of meat. "The view that in order to detect the unsoundness of this meat would require a resident analyst would not be supported by authority… It was not sufficient for the purposes of Section 308 to say Mr Hobbs could not have discovered it was injurious to health."

In a ruling that subsequently formed part of case law on the meaning of mens rea, the court allowed the appeal with costs and ruled that the sum of £918 be returned to Winchester Corporation.

*First published in Environmental Health News
on 30th July, 2010, page 36*

## APPENDIX FOUR

# The inspector who wouldn't be suppressed

*With its overcrowded housing and riverside towns, Kent was an incubator for disease in the 19th century. One determined sanitary inspector tracked down the cause of outbreaks of typhoid.*

Between 1851 and 1854, cholera killed 170 people in Tonbridge, Kent, which extracted its drinking water from the sewage-laden river Medway. Charles Dickens' brother, Alfred, a sanitary inspector, was sent by the General Board of Health to investigate.

His findings catalogued stagnant streams, dirty, unpaved roads, dung heaps, offensive cesspools and filthy premises. In 1855, Dickens wrote a celebrated report on conditions in cholera-ravaged West Ham, focusing on the parlous state of its sewers, drains and water supplies.

Cholera largely left Kent in the 1860s, but outbreaks of typhoid continued. In the 1890s, the disease struck Maidstone and Folkestone. The January 1911 Sanitary Journal contains a fascinating account of the role of Folkestone's sanitary inspector, John Pearson, in tracing the causes of the disease.

The tone of his article is somewhat bitter. It sheds interesting light on how sanitary inspectors interacted with the medical officers of health who directed their work, often in a lofty and high-handed fashion.

Recalling cases recorded 11 years before, in 1900, Pearson describes his puzzlement about why typhoid keeps returning to Folkestone. He investigates and discovers that sporadic outbreaks are linked to common milk suppliers (this was long before routine pasteurisation) and a common milker called "R".

He presents his hypothesis that "R" has something to do with the persistent typhoid, but his boss, an unnamed medical officer, will have nothing of it. He thinks it is the drains.

In 1901, the Local Government Board sends an investigator, Dr Theodore Thomson. His report on the cause of the typhoid is inconclusive — drains, shellfish, polluted water used by dairies. He also slaps down the impudent sanitary inspector for having strayed beyond his normal duties. He notes, "It is no part of the duties of an inspector of nuisances to report upon the etiology of questions involving medical considerations," and he castigates the council for letting the officer get above himself.

Happily, Mr Pearson continues his epidemiological research. Fortunately, a German scientist establishes that people who have contracted typhoid with no symptoms can spread the disease. Armed with this knowledge, Mr Pearson, who describes himself as "the inspector who wouldn't be suppressed", asks the Local Government Board to send a new investigator.

Dr R.W.Johnstone is despatched and finds Mr Pearson is correct. The milker "R" is indeed carrying a virulent typhoid bacillus. He writes that the value of Mr Pearson's investigations, conducted with "great intelligence and perseverance", is "fully admitted". But, as Mr Pearson observes, medical men tend not to criticise their own. Dr Johnstone does not upbraid Dr Thomson for dismissing the sanitary inspector and, instead, defends the earlier report.

Mr Pearson should be the hero of this tale. The celebrated disease carrier, "Typhoid Mary" claimed her first victims in the US in 1901, but she was not identified as the cause of outbreaks of typhoid until 1906. Hence, Mr Pearson's discovery of an asymptomatic carrier predates the US case by six years

He deserves to be remembered in history, for having, like Dr John Snow, stuck to an offbeat theory of disease causation in the face of opposition, disbelief and the possible loss of his job. However, it would appear that his touching story has never spread further than pages of The Sanitary Journal.

His article predicts his fate: "As the years go on, no doubt all references to [my] pioneer work will disappear from the literature dealing with typhoid fever, but it seems only right that the journal devoted to the interests of the sanitary inspector should give a detailed and accurate account of the part played by one of the members of their uninstructed and despised calling." Indeed. EHN is happy to put the record straight.

*First published in Environmental Health News*
*on 28th January, 2011, page 36*

# SOURCES

## Introduction

Acheson, D., Public Health in England Report, 1988

Brown, C. and Savage, C. (eds.) For the Common Good: 150 Years of Public Health: An EHJ commemorative issue, CIEH

Chiozza Money, L. G., Riches and Poverty, Methuen and Co., 1910

Dangerfield, G., The Strange Death of Liberal England, Macgibbon and Kee, 1966

Johnson, R. A., A Century of Progress: The History of the Institution of Environmental Health Officers 1883-1983, IEHO, 1983

Poulton, R., Kings and Commoners 1901-1936, World's Work, 1977

## The Public Health Traditions

Anon., Our Twenty-Seventh Annual Dinner: Full and Descriptive Report, The Sanitary Journal, February 1910, pp. 215-216

Crichton-Browne, Sir J., Account of the President's address at the 1910 annual dinner, The Sanitary Journal, February 1910, pp. 218-20

Derbyshire, D., Hatchett, W. and Turkington, R. (eds.) Taking Stock: Social Housing and the CIEH in the Twentieth Century, CIEH, 1996

Eastwood, M., "Liverpool: a town ahead of its time" in Brown, C. and Savage, C. (eds) For the Common Good: 150 Years of Public Health: An EHJ commemorative issue, CIEH

Mason, D., "Edwin Chadwick 1800-1899" in Brown, C. and Savage, C. (eds) For the Common Good: 150 Years of Public Health: An EHJ commemorative issue, CIEH

Maynard, E., Women in the Public Health Service, The Scientific Press, 1915

Neve, M. and Turner, T., What the doctor thought and did: Sir James Crichton-Browne, Medical History, 1995, 39, pp. 399-432

Simon, Sir J., English Sanitary Institutions: reviewed in their course of development and in some of their political and social relation, John Murray, 1897

Vacher, F., "The Modern Sanitary Inspector" in The Sanitary Journal, October 1910, pp. 150-152

## Poverty

Booth, C., "Life and Labour of the People of London" in Keating, P. (ed.) Into Unknown England 1866-1913, Fontana/Collins, 1978

Booth, W., "In Darkest England and the Way Out" in Keating, P. (ed.) Into Unknown England 1866-1913, Fontana/Collins, 1978

Carey, M., "Reports of the Poor Law Commissions" in The Sanitary Journal, January 1910, pp. 205-208

Fabian Society, A Plea for Poor Law Reform, Tract No. 44, 1894

Kent, W., John Burns: Labour's Lost Leader, Williams & Norgate, 1950

London, J., The People of the Abyss, The Journeyman Press, 1980

Poulton, R., Kings and Commoners 1901-1936, World's Work, 1977

Rowntree, B. S., "Poverty: A Study of Town Life" in Keating, P. (ed.) Into Unknown England 1866-1913, Fontana/Collins, 1978

Simon, Sir J., English Sanitary Institutions: reviewed in their course of development and in some of their political and social relations, John Murray, 1897

Squire, Rose E., Thirty Years in the Public Service, London, Nisbet & Co. Ltd, 1927

## Mills and Maladies

Annual Reports on the Health of Bradford by the Medical Officers of Health 1900 to 1911, published by the City of Bradford

Bourdan, A., Typhoid Mary, Bloomsbury Publishing plc, 2005

Roberts, L., Aids to Public Health, Balliere, Tindall & Cox, 1923-52

Wright, D. G. and Jowitt, J. A. (eds.) Victorian Bradford, CBMC, 1982

## The Women Inspectors

Bruley, S., Women in Britain since 1900, MacMillan Press Ltd.,1999

Carey, M., "The Whole Work of a Sanitary Inspector", The Sanitary Journal, March 1908, pp. 191-193  Chinn, C., They worked all their lives: women of the urban poor, 1880-1939, Manchester University Press, 1988

Chiozza Money, L. G., Riches and Poverty, Methuen and Co., 1910

Cowman, K., Women of the Right Spirit: paid organisers of the women's social and political union 1904-18, Manchester, Manchester University Press, 2011

 Crawford, E., The Women's Suffrage Movement: a reference guide 1866-1928, Routledge, 1999  Dangerfield, G., The Strange Death of Liberal England, Macgibbon and Kee, 1966

Davey Smith, G., Dorling, D. and Shaw M. (eds.) Poverty, inequality and health in Britain, 1800-2000: a reader, The Policy Press, 2001

Davies, C., "The Health Visitor as Mother's Friend: A Woman's place in public health, 1900-14" in Social History of Medicine 1, pp. 39-50, 1988

Dowling W., The Ladies Sanitary Association and the origins of the health visiting service, MA thesis, University of London, 1963

Harrison, B., Not only the dangerous trades: women's work and health in Britain, 1880-1914, Taylor & Francis, 1996

Holloway, G., Women and work in Britain since 1840, Routledge, 2005

Hutchins, B. L., The working life of women, Fabian Society, 1911

Kanner, B., Women in English social history, 1800-1914: a guide to research, Vol. 1, Garland Publishing Inc., 1988

Lawson, M., Memories of Charlotte Marsh, leaflet produced for the Suffragette Fellowship, 1961

Laybourn, K., The Guild of Help and the Changing Face of Edwardian Philanthropy, Edward Mellen Press, 1945

Maynard, E., Women in the Public Health Service, The Scientific Press, 1915

Maynard, E., "The Work of Women Sanitary Inspectors" in The Sanitary Journal, February 1911, pp. 240-242

McFeely, M. D., Lady Inspectors: the Campaign for a Better Workplace 1893-1921, Basil Blackwell, 1988

Oakley, A., Housewife, Penguin, 1974  Purvis, J. (ed.) Women's history: Britain 1850-1945 an introduction, Routledge, 2000

Raeburn, A., The Militant Suffragettes, New English Library, 1973

Sanders, V. and Delap, L., Victorian and Edwardian Anti-Feminism, Volumes I, II & III, Routledge, 2010

Saunders, Mrs, "Women in Public Health Administration" in The Sanitary Journal, May 1910, pp. 284-297

Shillito, A., "Letter to the Editor Opposing the Proposed Affiliation of Male and Female Sanitary Inspectors' Associations" in The Sanitary Journal, January 1910, p. 199

Squire, Rose E., Thirty Years in the Public Service, London, Nisbet & Co. Ltd, 1927

Vacher, F., "The Position of Women With Regard to Public Sanitary Work" in The Sanitary Journal, November 11, pp. 168-171

Woodfield, L., "Some Observations of a Health Missioner" in The Sanitary Journal, June 1907, pp. 5-7

## The Home

Bell, Y., The Edwardian Home, Shire Library, 2009

Benn, T., "An antidote to socialist despair" in The Guardian, 3rd February 2011

Briggs, A., Social History of England, Penguin, 1991

Casciani, D., "Is this the nicest place to live in Britain?" in BBC News Channel, 9th July 2003

Fabian Society, The Tenant's Sanitary Catechism (for places outside London), Tract No. 68, 1896

Fabian Society, Houses for the People. A summary of the powers of local authorities under the Housing of the Working Classes Acts, 1890 to 1900, Tract No. 76, 1900

Forster, M., Hidden Lives: a family memoire, Penguin, 2010

Herbert, I., "Rowntree Idealism Lives On In New Model Village" in The Independent, 4th July 1999

Hibbert, C., The English: A Social History 1066-1945, Paladin Grafton Books, 1987

Hilditch, M., "Home Sweet Home?" in Inside Housing, 29th January 2010

Marr, A., The Making of Modern Britain from Queen Victoria to V.E. Day, Macmillan, 2009

Tressell, R., The Ragged Trousered Philanthropists, Lawrence Wishart, 1955

Wohl, A., The Eternal Slum: Housing and Social Policy in Victorian London, Edward Arnold, 1977

Yorke, T., The Edwardian House Explained, Countryside Books, 2006

## Planning

Addison, A., The Betrayal of the Slums, H. Jenkins, 1922

Anon. "Visit to Letchworth (Sanitary Inspector's South-Eastern Centre)" in The Sanitary Journal, November 1905, pp. 164-165

Bell, Y., The Edwardian Home, Shire Library, 2009

Grant, C. (ed.) Built to Last? Reflections on British Housing Policy, Roof, 1992

Hattersley, R., The Edwardians, Time Warner Group Ltd, 2004

Hibbert, C., The English: A Social History 1066-1945, Paladin Grafton Books, 1987

Hounsell, P., Ealing and Hanwell Past, Historical Publications Ltd, 2010

Howard, E., To-morrow: a Peaceful Path to Real Reform 1898 and Garden Cities of Tomorrow, 1902 (reprinted by Faber and Faber, 1946)

Lowe, R., "Looking Forward: Paper read at meeting of North Wales Centre by Robert Lowe, Sanitary Inspector, Rhyl, 18th February, 1911" in The Sanitary Journal, March 1911, pp. 266-7

Miller, M., Letchworth Garden City Pocket Images, Nonsuch, 1995

Miller, M., English Garden Cities: an introduction, English Heritage, 2010

Unwin, R. and Parker, B., Cottage Plans and Common Sense, Tract No. 68, Fabian Society, 1902

Snow, L., Willesden Past, Phillimore, 1994

Yorke, T., The Edwardian House Explained, Countryside Books, 2006

# Food

Anon., "Visit to Messrs Peak and Frean's Biscuit Works" and "Visit to Messrs, Otto Monsted Ltd's Margarine Factory" in The Sanitary Journal, September 1910, pp. 70-71

Atkins, P. J., "The Glasgow case: meat, disease and regulation, 1889-1924", Agricultural History Review, 52 (2), pp. 161-182

Booth, C., "Life and Labour of the People of London" in Keating, P. (ed.) Into Unknown England 1866-1913, Fontana/Collins, 1978

Booth, W., "In Darkest England and the Way out" in Keating, P. (ed.) Into Unknown England 1866-1913, Fontana/Collins, 1978

Crichton-Browne, Sir J., "Account of the President's Address at the 1910 Annual Dinner" in The Sanitary Journal, February 1910, pp. 218-20

Fylde, P., "Sanitary Control of the Milk Supply" in The Sanitary Journal, July 1910, pp. 29-30

London, J., The People of the Abyss, The Journeyman Press, 1980

Niven, J., Observations of the History of Public Health Effort in Manchester, John Heywood Ltd, 1923

Pember Reeves, Mrs, "Family Life on a Pound a Week" in Keating, P. (ed.) Into Unknown England 1866-1913, Fontana/Collins, 1978

Phillips, J. and French, M., "State Regulation and Hazards of Milk, 1900-1939" in Social History of Medicine, Volume 12, Issue 3, pp. 371-388

Robinson, J. A., "The Need For A More Comprehensive Inspection Of Food" in The Sanitary Journal, October, 1911, pp. 147-151

Rowntree, B. S., "Poverty: A Study of Town Life" in Keating, P. (ed.) Into Unknown England 1866-1913, Fontana/Collins, 1978

## Mental health

Arnold C., Bedlam, Great Britain, Simon & Schuster UK Ltd, 2008

Barker, D., How to Curb the Fertility of the Unfit: the feeble minded in Edwardian Britain, Oxford Review of Education, Volume 9, No 3, 1983

Bewley, T., Madness to Mental Illness. A History of the Royal College of Psychiatrists, RCPsych Publications, 2008

British Medical Association, "Ninety First Annual Meeting, July 1923" in The British Medical Journal, 11th August 1923, pp. 219-234

British Medical Journal, "National Association For the Promoting The Welfare of the Feeble Minded" in British Medical Journal, 14th July 1900

British Medical Journal, "The Report of the Royal Commission on the Feeble Minded" in British Medical Journal, 15th August 1908

Jackson, M., The Borderland of Imbecility, Manchester University Press, 2000

Joseph Rowntree Foundation, Contemporary Social Evils, The Policy Press, University of Bristol, 2009

Jackson, M., Menace to the Good of Society: Class, Fertility and the Feeble-Minded in Edwardian England, Department of History, University of Exeter, 2004

MacDonald, M., Madness Anxiety and Healing in Seventeenth Century England, Cambridge University Press, 1983

Schama, S., A History of Britain 1776-2000, BBC Worldwide Ltd., 2002

Scull, A., Museums of Madness Revisited, The Society for the Social History of Medicine, 1993

Simmons, H.G., "Explaining social policy: The English Mental Deficiency Act of 1913" in Journal of Social History, Vol: 11, No 3, pp. 387 - 403

## The Workhouse

Englander, D., Poverty and Poor Law Reform in 19th Century Britain, 1834-1914, Pearson Education Limited, 1998

Freeman, M., "Journeys into poverty kingdom: complete participation and the British vagrant, 1866-1914" in History Workshop Journal (52), pp. 99-121, 2001

Hay, J.R., The Origins of the Liberal Welfare Reforms 1906-1914. 1987, Macmillan Education Ltd., 1975

Higginbotham, P., Life in a Victorian Workhouse 1834 to 1930, Pitkin publishing, 2011

Higgs, M., Life In The Victorian and Edwardian Workhouse, The History Press, 2009

London, J., The People of the Abyss, The Journeyman Press, 1980

Rees, R., Poverty and Public Health 1815-1948, Heinemann Educational Publishers, 2001

Thane, P., "The Working Class and State Welfare in Britain 1880-1914" in Gladstone, D. (ed.) Before Beveridge: Welfare Before the Welfare State, The Cromwell Press, 1999, pp. 86-113,

Vincent, A. W., "The Poor Law Reports on 1909" and "The Social Theory of the Charity Organisation Society" in Gladstone, D. (ed.) Before Beveridge: Welfare Before the Welfare State, The Cromwell Press, 1999, pp. 64-85

Ward, M., Beatrice Webb: her quest for a fairer society. A hundred years of the minority report, The Smith Institute, 2011

## Port Health

Cook, G. C., "Letter from 'An Old Inspector'" in The Sanitary Journal, May 1910, p. 282

Disease in the Merchant Navy, a History of the Seaman's Hospital Society, Oxford, Radcliffe Publishing Ltd, 2007

Foskett, E. W., "International Aspects". Chapter 2 of Bassett, W. H. (ed.), Clay's Handbook of Environmental Health, Sixteenth Edition, London, 1992, pp. 32-42

Hanna, W., Report on Marine Hygiene: being suggestions for improvements in the sanitary arrangements and appliances on shipboard, Liverpool Port Sanitary Authority, 1917

Hardy, A., Cholera, Quarantine and the English Preventive System 1850-1895, Medical History 37, 1993, pp. 250-269

Hope, R. A., New History of British Shipping, John Murray, Chapter 18, 1990, pp. 331-348

Kemp, P., The British Sailor: a social history of the lower deck, Dent, 1970

Maglen, K., "The First Line of Defence: British Quarantine and the Port Sanitary Authorities in the Nineteenth Century" in The Society for the Social History of Medicine, Vol. 15, 2002, pp. 413-428

Mitchell, A., "Plague in South Africa: Perpetuation and Spread of Infection by Wild Rodents", read at South African Medical Congress, Cape Town, 9th October, 1921

Mole, R. K. K., "Of Rats, Fleas, And Peoples: Towards A History Of Bubonic Plague In Southern Africa, 1890-1950" in Botswana Journal of African Studies, Vol. 15, No. 5, 2001   Port of London Authority, First Annual Report with Accounts for the year ended 31 March, 1910

Rees, H., British ports and Shipping, G. G. Harrap, 1958

Rotheram, P., "Port Health". Chapter 12 of Bassett, W. H. (ed.) Clay's Handbook of Environmental Health, Sixteenth Edition, London, 1992, pp. 180-194

Sheard, S., "Mixed Motives: improving the health of seamen in Liverpool 1875-1939" in Abreu, L. (ed.) European Health and Social Welfare Policies, Compostela Group of Universities, 2004, pp. 321-336

Shrewsbury, J. F. D., A History of Bubonic Plague in the British Isles, Cambridge University Press, 2005

Smedley, John H. M., Practical Ship and Port Sanitation, The Sanitary Publishing Company Limited, London, undated

## Useful websites

**www.apha.org.uk/history.html**
Association of Port Health Authorities

**www.bbc.co.uk/history**
General resources, including a useful overview of social and medical themes in the Victorian and Edwardian periods

**www.brentham.com**
Brentham garden suburb, Ealing

**www.british-history.ac.uk**
British history online – a compendious archive, good on municipal and government records relating to public health pre-20th century

**www.1911census.co.uk**
Access to the last available census

**www.cieh.org**
The Chartered Institute of Environmental Health

**www.cityoflondon.gov.uk**
London Metropolitan Archives, holding the records of the City of London Corporation and the former Greater London Council and London County Council

**www.ehn-online.com**
Environmental Health News, the monthly journal of the CIEH

**www.gardencitymuseum.org**
First Garden City Heritage Museum, Letchworth, Hertfordshire

**www.hgs.org.uk/history/index.html**
Hampstead garden suburb

**www.hullandgoolepha.gov.uk**
Hull and Goole Port Health Authority

**www.londonmet.ac.uk**
Includes the Trades Union Congress library collections and the women's library, celebrating and recording women's lives

**www2.lse.ac.uk**
London School of Economics. Pamphlets and tracts relating to social and political history, including the Fabian Society online archive

**www.mersey-gateway.org**
History of the Liverpool Port Health Authority

**www.movinghere.org.uk**
Migration histories for the Caribbean, Irish, Jewish and South Asian communities

**www.nationalarchives.gov.uk**
A comprehensive archive of resources including government and personal papers, some accessible online

**www.ph.ucla.edu**
University of California Los Angeles, School of Public Health. Good on disease and epidemiology in late-Victorian London

**www.pla.co.uk/centenary**
Port of London website, celebrating its centenary

**www.rsph.org.uk**
Royal Society for Public Health

**www.victorianweb.org**
Wide range of useful historical resources on the pre-Edwardian era

**www.winstonchurchill.org**
Website of the Churchill Centre and Museum, including papers and speeches

**www.workhouses.org.uk**
Comprehensive site, described as a mixture of social history, politics, economics and architecture

## Photographs

Page 12: Edward G. Brewis/The Sanitary Journal 1910

Page 22: Hulton Archive/Getty

Page 33 and cover: Copyright Bradford Museum Galleries

Page 47: Lewis W. Hine/Archive/Getty

Page 64: Jon Heal/CIEH

Page 70: First Garden City Heritage Museum, Letchworth

Page 72: First Garden City Heritage Museum, Letchworth

Page 78: William Hatchett/CIEH

Page 87: Bob Thomas/Popperfoto/Getty

Page 102: Topical Press Agency/Getty

Page 113: GPA/Hulton Picture Archive/Getty

Page 124: Hulton Archive/Getty

Back cover: Bill Carey, family collection

# THE AUTHORS

**DR STEPHEN BATTERSBY** was born in Liverpool and took his first degree in chemistry and applied zoology. He trained as a public health inspector in his native city. He worked for several local authorities before becoming assistant secretary to the then Environmental Health Officers Association in 1980. An independent environmental health and housing consultant, Stephen is an associate of the World Health Organization's collaborating centre on housing standards and was a member of the team that developed the housing health and safety rating system. He is the current editor of Clay's Handbook of Environmental Health. He is a fellow of the CIEH and the Royal Society for Public Health and a past CIEH chair and president.

Born in Nottingham, **DAVID CLAPHAM** was until recently environmental health manager for City of Bradford Metropolitan Council. Now a consultant, he has worked in environmental health for nearly 40 years. His main interest is in safe drinking water and he was a founder of the Water for Kids charity. David has published Small Water Supplies: A Practical Guide, Spon Press, 2004, as well as contributing chapters to expert reference works. In his spare time, he has an allotment, does swimming, spinning, reading, taking music-baths and caring for three big children. He is a DJ for his local BCB radio station. He is a Fellow of the Royal Society for Public Health and a member of the Chartered Institute of Environmental Health.

**TIM EVERETT** qualified as an EHO in 1977 and initially worked on poor housing in central London before moving to environmental protection and commercial regulation in London and Swansea. He played a lead role as borough EHO in developing Sutton's environmental policies and was a national adviser to local government associations on air quality and contaminated land. He was a strategic director at Worthing BC from 2003 and then, jointly, of Worthing and Adur DCs. Tim became CIEH executive director of professional services in 2009. He holds qualifications in law and housing. He is a fellow of the RSPH, a chartered member of the Chartered Institute of Housing, and a fellow and chartered practitioner of the CIEH. He is committed to supporting the Samaritans and his local Citizens Advice Bureau.

**AVA GREENWELL**'s first degree was in law and politics. She worked in a couple of mental hospitals and moved to work on a mammoth history of fashion and other publications, including some alternative newspapers, The Observer and the Financial Times. She then helped to run an organic smallholding and got the environmental "bug". Intrigued, she studied environmental science (at her own expense) and had a spell working in environmental health before moving on to recycling, then industrial waste minimisation, and finally voluntary regulation, completing at the London School of Economics a PhD examining institutional aspects of resource efficiency. She has two grown-up children and a very tolerant, lovely husband.

**WILLIAM HATCHETT** was born in Oxford. He studied at the universities of Bangor, North Wales, and Paris VIII, and the London College of Printing, and has been a journalist for 25 years. He has written for many publications, including The Guardian, New Society and the New Statesman and has worked on professional publications including Community Care, Voluntary Housing and Housing magazines. Currently, he is editor of Environmental Health News, the magazine of the Chartered Institute of Environmental Health. He lives in London close to his daughter and two grandsons. His hobbies are messing about with canoes and playing the guitar. He is the author of Rural Drives: a journey through English housing policy, York Publishing Services, 1999.

**STUART SPEAR** was born in Paris and studied psychology and anthropology at London University. After working in the City for 10 years, he retrained as a journalist at the London College of Printing. He has been writing about public and environmental health for 15 years, seven of them spent editing Environmental Health Practitioner, the Chartered Institute of Environmental Health's monthly journal. He is married with three children and currently lives in south London where he works as a freelance journalist. He has recently authored research on wellbeing for the Department of Health and contributed to a number of books on wellbeing and public health.

**JILL STEWART** grew up on the outskirts of Greater London and spent much of her childhood on housing estates where her experiences of good and bad policy have had a profound effect on her current views and work in environmental health. Having studied in London and Bristol, she now teaches at the University of Greenwich across public health and housing programmes and has written and co-written three books, several chapters and numerous journal papers. She is fascinated by amazing people in history; by the interrelationships between progress in health and science, art and design; and by how social history and literature can communicate the importance of public and environmental health more widely.

**JIM STEWART**'s varied and wide-ranging careers have led to his current lecturing post at Bucks New University where he combines his training in exacting arts and crafts standards of workmanship with teaching designer-makers. Subjects taught include aspects of art, design, craftsmanship and cultural theory, including the importance of the built environment and its context, from the arts and crafts movement to beyond post modernism. Combining work and pleasure, and having driven to Poland and to within sight of Africa in his VW, his recent research investigated the camper van and how to make better use of a small living space – ironically now an important element of overcrowded housing.